Lean Knowledge Management

Lean Knowledge Management

How NASA Implemented a Practical KM Program

Roger Forsgren

BEP

BUSINESS EXPERT PRESS

Leader in applied, concise business books

First published in 2021 by
Business Expert Press, LLC
222 East 46th Street, New York, NY 10017
www.businessexpertpress.com

ISBN-13: 978-1-63742-133-8 (paperback)
ISBN-13: 978-1-63742-134-5 (e-book)

Business Expert Press Portfolio and Project Management Collection

Collection ISSN: 2156-8189 (print)
Collection ISSN: 2156-8200 (electronic)

First edition: 2021

10 9 8 7 6 5 4 3 2 1

Description

***Lean Knowledge Management* Helped Change NASA's Culture and It Can Do the Same for Your Organization**

NASA suffered three human spaceflight tragedies and *Lean Knowledge Management was a major tool that helped NASA management implement massive cultural changes.*

Traditional knowledge management is too often regarded as overly complicated or a wasteful bureaucratic exercise, but *Lean Knowledge Management can become a critical component for your organization to operate effectively, efficiently and safely.*

Lean Knowledge Management simplifies the process by:

- Clearly defining your organization's key employees.
- Filtering the enormous amount of internal "information" into "critical knowledge".
- Utilizing a myriad of resources to get this critical knowledge to the people who need it most—the very people that can make your organization successful.

Repetitive mistakes and failures can cost an organization millions of dollars in lost revenue, scrap, and even lawsuits. Lean Knowledge Management strips away the academic jargon and implements a practical, cost-effective, organic program emphasizing lessons of the past.

Knowledge is free! Your hard-earned corporate knowledge is *right in front of you*, why risk losing it and having to pay for it all over again?

Knowledge is power! Lean Knowledge Management is a structured plan to harness that power for your organization.

Keywords

lean knowledge management; knowledge management; engineering training; NASA; lessons learned; learning from the past; chief knowledge officer; sharing knowledge; case studies; Apollo 1 accident; Shuttle Challenger; Shuttle Columbia; technical authority

Contents

Testimonials

"Too often, Knowledge Management has been seen as a somewhat confusing and ineffective process, but now Roger Forsgren unravels the complexities and clearly demonstrates how an organization's culture can be transformed. By focusing on critical knowledge and utilizing the practical tools described in Lean Knowledge Management, any organization, even a research and development one, can reduce overall costs, gain process efficiencies, product reliability, and grow customer satisfaction. This powerful tool helped transform NASA by learning the difficult lessons of its past and it can help any organization develop a culture of safety, efficiency, and dependability."—**Dr. Andrew Liou, Executive Vice President, Foxconn Technology Group**

"Knowledge has to be captured and then transferred to a new project where it can be used. Project professionals need to be trained in its use. Roger Forsgren's delightful book clearly explains how NASA achieved that."—**Dr. Rodney Turner, Former President and Chairman at International Project Management Association**

"I've been following Roger and his team's work at NASA starting with APPEL well over a decade ago…and to this day, I often refer, (and refer others), to it for guidance and best practices. What has resonated with me from the beginning was its simplicity and common sense approach toward capturing and sharing knowledge—using a creative mix of formal, informal interventions based on maximizing peer-to-peer collaboration. This book IS a blueprint for anyone starting and operating a robust KM model in their organization without the complexities."—**Jerry Colello, Director–Knowledge Management, Pratt & Whitney Aircraft, Raytheon Technologies Corporation**

"Roger explains a lean, practical, and engineer-proven way to implement Knowledge Management in an organization. Using examples from NASA and human history, he shows the importance of gathering and sharing important information with the people who need it. This makes the book easy to read and special. A must-read for any manager."—**Uwe Knodt, Head of Strategic Services, Deutsches Zentrum für Luft- und Raumfahrt (DLR), DLR (German Aerospace Center)**

"The new world is one based on knowledge. Lean KM offers a practical approach to Knowledge Management, filled with historical references and interesting stories. It brought back wonderful memories of NASA."—**Dr. Edward J Hoffman Former, NASA CKO and Director of the NASA Academy of Program, Project, & Engineering Leadership (APPEL), CEO Knowledge Strategies LLC Lecturer, Columbia University, Information and Knowledge Strategy (IKNS)**

Preface

I have always had a love for history and majored in it at Georgetown University, despite my father's warnings that I'd never find a decent job. Several years after graduating, and after not being able to find a decent job, I decided to start all over and applied at NASA as an apprentice mechanic. I spent the next decade learning how to use a lathe, torque wrench, TIG welder, and bend tubing while going to night school to earn an engineering degree, yet history remained my first love.

I spent 38 years working at the National Aeronautics and Space Administration. After starting as an apprentice mechanic at the Lewis Research Center (now the Glenn Research Center) in Cleveland, Ohio, I ended my career as the agency's chief knowledge officer at NASA Headquarters in Washington, DC.

During my career at NASA, I had the opportunity to serve in almost every role on a project team: technician, discipline engineer, deputy manager, and project manager. I flew in the *Vomit Comet* (and, yes, vomited), I spent almost two weeks working inside the Space Shuttle Columbia's payload bay to install an experiment, I earned a patent, some of my handiwork flew in space (with my children's initials delicately and surreptitiously scratched into the iridited aluminum), and I spent a career working with some of the smartest and most dedicated people in the world. At NASA, you can learn something new every day. It really was a job that I looked forward to each day. NASA is a wonderful place that appreciates and rewards hard work; I went from a wage grade pay level to a senior leader (SL) position.

When I was named chief knowledge officer, I was able to combine my engineering knowledge and my years of program and project experience with my love for history. It was a unique opportunity to utilize an engineer's pragmatic, focused perspective with the critical thinking skills of an historian. It was an unaccustomed combination of the sciences with liberal arts. Forty years after graduating, it was also an opportunity to show my Dad I could finally use my history degree!

Being the NASA chief knowledge officer may have been a bit daunting at the time, but it was also a wonderful experience. I was fortunate to lead an extraordinary team of skilled professionals, and together, we designed, developed, and implemented the program described in the following pages: lean knowledge management.

Acknowledgments

After 38 years at NASA, there are just too many individuals I have had the pleasure to know and learn from than can possibly be listed here, but I would like to thank my mentors and good friends at NASA Headquarters: Ed Hoffman and Hal Bell.

I would also like thank Stephen Angelillo and the entire APPEL team for their hard work and dedication in helping develop a lean knowledge management program for NASA.

A special thanks is owed to Donna Wilson, whose understanding of training and KM every NASA employee is indebted; Dan Connell for his ability to transform vague requirements into creative IT accomplishments; Jenn Sizemore and Kevin Magee for helping develop the future leaders that will help place the next Americans on the Moon and then Mars; and Dan Daly and Ramien Pierre for their steady craftsmanship and dedication that ensures critical knowledge is shared throughout the agency.

In particular, I owe a great deal of appreciation to Susan Snyder, Rob Clairmont, Dr. Moses Adoko, and my wife, Florence, for proofreading this manuscript and providing excellent suggestions and enhancements.

Introduction

In a *Wall Street Journal* article, not long ago, the author stated that "… knowledge management isn't dead, but it's gasping for breath.[1]" I believe it's gasping for a breath for two reasons, we've made it much more complicated than it needs to be and we've failed to demonstrate what an enormous, positive effect a strong KM program can have on an organization's success. For companies trying to compete in a dog-eat-dog marketplace where the bottom line dictates an organization's funding priorities, an effective KM program needs to be recognized as a critical tool—not an additional layer of bureaucracy, complexity, or cost—that can help organizations become successful and profitable in a world where only the strong survive.

There are countless academic books out there defining knowledge management, in terms to the layman, that can appear almost incomprehensible and obscure. The goal of this book is not a complicated thesis explaining knowledge management, but rather, a practical book describing how a team at NASA defined what KM means to the NASA workforce and implemented a program that was designed around engineering principles for simplicity, efficiency, and effectiveness. It is a manual describing how to implement such a program in any organization.

Knowledge management at NASA has been an arduous journey. It started in 2011 when the Aerospace Safety Advisory Panel (ASAP), a distinguished group of experts from the aeronautics and space sectors that are appointed by Congress to advise NASA's management about space and aeronautics operations, recommended NASA appoint a chief knowledge officer. Their report to the NASA administrator stated: "To ensure the identification and capture of critical NASA implicit and explicit knowledge, the ASAP recommends NASA establish a single focal point (a Chief Knowledge Officer) within the Agency to develop the policy

---

[1] Davenport, T. January 24, 2015. "Whatever Happened to Knowledge Management?" *The Wall Street Journal, CIO Report*.

and requirements necessary *to integrate knowledge capture across programs, projects, and Centers* [my italics].[2]"

NASA moved forward with this recommendation and did an exceptional job at gathering lessons and case studies throughout the agency but was having challenges disseminating this critical knowledge to the people within the agency that needed it most. In 2014, the ASAP stated in its report that the panel, "…strongly recommends a continuous and formal effort in knowledge capture and lessons learned. *Modern tools exist* [my italics] to facilitate this, and NASA should avail itself of them. Rigor in this area is particularly critical as the experience in specific skills dissipates over time and as engineering talent is stretched across programs.[3]"

For several years, the ASAP monitored NASA's KM program, and although much impressed with the quality and amount of knowledge gathered, the panel was still frustrated that this critical knowledge wasn't getting to the NASA workforce. In their 2016 report to Congress, they stated: "The Panel has not been encouraged by the response to its recommendation on Knowledge Capture and Lessons Learned. The ASAP has strongly recommended a continuous and formal effort in knowledge capture that is *highly visible and easily accessible* [my italics]. Initial efforts… appeared promising but have failed to date to result in an Agency-wide, effective process.[4]" They placed KM for NASA in a *red* status, meaning they had serious concerns and believed corrective actions were needed. This was certain to get the attention of *The Ninth Floor* where the NASA administrator and other high-powered managers resided.

At the time, I wasn't much involved with knowledge management as I was the director of the Academy of Program/Project and Engineering Leadership (APPEL) and responsible for project management and systems engineering training for the agency. Other than occasionally reviewing a lessons learned entry in our database or reading an interesting case study, I didn't know much about knowledge management. It's not like I didn't try. I read books about it and sat through many academic-type

---

[2] https://oiir.hq.nasa.gov/asap/documents/2011_ASAP_Annual_Report.pdf
[3] https://oiir.hq.nasa.gov/asap/documents/ASAP_Public_Meeting_Minutes_1st-qtr-2014.pdf
[4] https://oiir.hq.nasa.gov/asap/documents/2016_ASAP_Annual_Report.pdf

lectures on knowledge management, but I simply couldn't decipher what practical benefits could be gained from many of the esoteric (and to me, confusing) models presented. The authors and lecturers, all without a doubt very intelligent, were making knowledge management too complicated and were presenting an approach that seemed simply too impractical. I just couldn't find a blueprint for a KM framework that I thought would resonate with the engineers, scientists, and technicians of the NASA workforce.

So, as good engineers and project managers, we decided to go back to the beginning and review our design requirements. In the words of the ASAP, they wanted:

- An agency-wide KM program "…to integrate knowledge capture across programs, projects, and Centers."
- That included a, "formal effort in knowledge capture that is highly visible and easily accessible."
- And we were to use, "modern tools" to accomplish knowledge sharing.

After reviewing these requirements, I believe the most important course correction we took was twofold: defining exactly who our customers were within NASA and combining our knowledge management office with our very successful training and development program, APPEL. Focusing on, "knowledge capture across programs, projects, and Centers" clearly established the technical workforce, those involved in programs and projects at the NASA centers, as our customers, and once our customers have been defined, we knew precisely what type of knowledge we needed to gather. By utilizing our training office, which was, "highly visible and easily accessible" and all their resources and "modern tools" gave us the conduit we needed to get this knowledge to the right folks. Combing training with knowledge management was a crucial step in designing a lean KM program because it gave knowledge management the credibility it needed with the workforce, as well as an existing infrastructure allowing us to share knowledge with thousands of NASA employees.

Previously, we were good at gathering knowledge, but as the ASAP pointed out, we didn't have in place the KM infrastructure to efficiently disseminate this knowledge to the workforce. By joining our training office, we now had an established and respected program that could reach thousands of NASA employees each year through courses and a wide variety of learning events.

In addition to my role as the APPEL director, I was then appointed NASA's chief knowledge officer.

NASA is composed almost completely of a technical workforce who, by their nature, base their personal inclinations and professional skills on efficiency, practicality, and quality. I was determined to develop a program that would resonate with the NASA workforce and bring real, tangible value to those employees dedicated to our nation's space and aeronautics program.

Space exploration is a hard, unforgiving business. If any organization can benefit from the lessons of the past, it's NASA. What we did was remove the more quixotic concepts of what knowledge management is supposed to be and formed our own vision of what it could be if it were designed solely to meet the requirements of our workforce. In essence, we developed a KM program that could survive the traditional engineering cost/benefits analysis. We worked to ensure the cost of developing a KM program was going to be worth our effort and worth the time and attention of our technical workforce.

Like good engineering, we designed a KM program that was robust yet simple. Everything has a specific function without any redundancy or unnecessary components. We designed a program that helps our workforce do their very difficult job and one whose cost can easily be justified in upper management's view. We made *lean knowledge management*.

I presented this vision of lean KM and, after three years of either being in the *yellow* or *red* status, the ASAP finally moved our program to *green*. In their annual report, they wrote in the typical straightforward style of an oversight committee: "The Panel received a briefing from NASA Chief Knowledge Officer at the second quarterly meeting of 2017, detailing the tools for sharing information. With the updates made to the Knowledge Management system, the ASAP closed this recommendation.[5]" Despite

---

[5] https://oiir.hq.nasa.gov/asap/documents/2017_ASAP_Annual_Report.pdf

their restrained language, my team and I were thrilled to get this episode behind us and move forward building our KM program.

I'm proud to say that the knowledge management program we put in place at NASA has been recognized, not only throughout the federal government, but also internationally as one of the very best. NASA learned to embrace KM the hard way; it took two shuttle tragedies and the loss of 14 exceptional astronauts before we understood how critical it is to share knowledge. Smart, effective, and practical knowledge management is one of the tools that helped transformed NASA's culture, and I strongly believe it can do the same for your organization.

As NASA's chief knowledge officer, I had been contacted by numerous federal and local government agencies as well as private industries who want to know how they can start a knowledge management program or get a fledging one off the ground. I had also listened to a lot of unique problems each agency or company had while trying to implement knowledge management. I hope to address these issues in the following pages and demonstrate why knowledge management is not only critical for a government agency such as NASA but can also provide powerful advantages for a business to become successful in an ever more competitive international marketplace.

NASA is a science and engineering organization, and these types of people are trained to design systems as simple and as effective as possible. "It just works" is every technical person's design goal. I modeled our KM program to reflect our customers, the NASA technical workforce. You will not find a lot of academic discussions about the theory of knowledge or abstract debates about epistemology in this book. You will find a simple, straightforward (i.e., lean) description of how we developed lean knowledge management, a knowledge program at NASA that *just works*.

CHAPTER 1

How Knowledge Management Helped Change NASA's Culture

On the afternoon of January 27, 1967, with less than three years left to accomplish President Kennedy's goal of landing an American on the Moon, astronauts Gus Grissom, Roger Chaffe, and Ed White climbed into the Apollo Command and Service Module (CSM) capsule atop a Saturn rocket at Cape Canaveral's Complex 34 for a launch rehearsal test.

Astronaut Grissom, at one point became so frustrated with the continual communication problems and garbled voices he heard through his headset, yelled into his microphone, "How are we going to get to the moon if we can't talk between two or three buildings?"

Suddenly, less than a minute after Grissom's outburst, a stunned Mission Control could hear Ed White suddenly yell, "Fire!" and then Gus Grissom screamed into his headset, "I've got a fire in the cockpit!" followed by a last, haunting scream, "Get us out of here!"

One of the men in mission control that afternoon was Flight Operations Director Chris Kraft who years later recounted, "It was terrible, I could hear all three of their voices, they didn't last very long either, about 10 or 15 seconds.[1]" During the launch rehearsal, a spark under the control panel, probably caused by a faulty wire assembly, almost instantly ignited the oxygen-rich air to over 10,000°F and incinerated the three astronauts. But Kraft explained the real cause of the tragedy that completely shook the National Aeronautics and Space Administration (NASA) and the Apollo program, "The management was running, running to get to the Moon and I think they were willing to take chances. I think had

---

[1] From the documentary, "Armstrong." Produced by Gravitas Ventures.

they been thinking properly they wouldn't have taken them.[2]" Decades afterward, Kraft somberly reflected, "I think we killed those men. It's almost murder.[3]"

NASA came into being in 1958 as a result of the launch of the first man-made satellite, Sputnik, by the Soviet Union. The American people, politicians, and military personnel were shocked and embarrassed to find their country so far behind Soviet technology. Within the context of the nuclear age, they were also terrified that this unforeseen scientific and engineering triumph by their bitter rival might increase the already dangerous Cold War. President Eisenhower transformed the old wartime National Advisory Committee for Aeronautics (NACA) into a new federal agency, NASA, which was immediately tasked with developing an answer to the Soviet Union's spectacular technical feat.

Two years after its founding, President Kennedy set the bar even higher, significantly higher, by tasking NASA to land a man on the moon and return him safely to Earth within the decade. An incredible technological challenge, but it had more of a political goal than a scientific or engineering objective. NASA was tasked to demonstrate the U.S.' technological prowess and show the world that American democracy and freedom could surpass Russian communism. The stakes were spectacularly high.

In only eight years—from its beginning in 1958 to 1966, at the height of the Apollo program, NASA went from NACA's original 8,000 employees to a staggering 420,000 (civil servants and contractor). Its budget went from $100 million to almost $6 billion (a 6,000 percent increase) and represented almost 4.5 percent of the entire federal budget. Today, NASA's budget is less the one-half of 1 percent of the federal budget. (Americans spend more money on pet food and pizza than on their space program!)

Within this context—starting almost from scratch and being thrown into a space race with the Soviets to show the world American technological and political power—NASA management was facing enormous

---

[2] Ibid.
[3] From the documentary, "Mission Control, the Unsung Heroes of Apollo." Produced by Gravitas Ventures.

Figure 1.1 The abandoned Launch Complex 34 where the Apollo I accident occurred. NASA has place historical markers for employees to reflect on the tragedy

pressures to fulfill President Kennedy's promise, and, after his assassination, found itself having to fulfill his legacy.

In order to accomplish such a monumental goal, NASA had to be managed with a hierarchical military-type chain of command. Money may no longer have been a factor, but time was of the essence because even the CIA couldn't determine the real status of the Soviet space program or how much further ahead their moon landing program may have been.

After the Apollo I tragedy, congressional inquiries discovered documents that appeared to show NASA managers and contractors may have suppressed their concerns over the safety and reliability of the CSM design in order to meet their inflexible flight schedule. Numerous congressman and senators scrutinized the way NASA was managing the Moon program as well as their insular management style and their unwillingness, or even their inability, to communicate openly and honestly with Congress.

NASA did learn a costly lesson, as Chris Kraft admitted that the accident forced NASA management to fix the design problems inherent in the CSM. "Without the Apollo I tragedy, we'd never have gotten to the Moon. I think that was the secret to Apollo. It took a fire to rebuild the vehicle, and I think that was the secret to Apollo.[4]" The Apollo program's technical problems may have been solved on July 20, 1969, when NASA delivered on President Kennedy's promise as Astronaut Neil Armstrong set foot on the Moon, but management and cultural issues within the agency would persist for decades afterward.

The Apollo Program came to an end in 1972, but the political and schedule pressures that NASA had been dealing with since its inception actually grew stronger. Now, with the country achieving its goal of a moon landing, NASA had to define its raison d'être to a Congress dealing with the Vietnam War as well as internal racial and political strife. The space program, once seen as America's proudest achievement, was now taking massive budget cuts, and NASA managers were desperately looking for a new program to justify the agency's existence.

That new program became the Space Transportation System (STS) or better known as the Space Shuttle Program. NASA, once again, had a major human spaceflight program along with the managerial stress that such a publicly prominent, costly, and incredibly technically complicated program brings. The program may have changed, but NASA's culture remained the same. In the two decades since the loss of the Apollo I crew, and now with the onset of such an enormous new program, NASA maintained a "Go Fever" management style that was willing to, at times, compromise engineering and overlook safety risks in order to get the program up and running.

Always under pressure from Congress to cut costs, NASA management in the early 1990s instituted the "Better, Faster, Cheaper" philosophy, which was supposed to help cut costs without sacrificing quality or performance. Certainly, a tall order. "Better, Faster, Cheaper" was never successful in the highly technical aerospace industry, and particularly within NASA. So much of NASA's work is based on cutting-edge research, which can be inherently expensive and isn't always schedule-driven. It's not unusual for some projects to be approved and funded despite the required technology not yet even existing. The projects are expected to invent new technologies in order to meet their requirements. Not really a

---

[4] Ibid.

suitable environment for "Better Faster Cheaper." (I can remember visiting NASA machine shops where technicians, those front-line, down-to-earth folks who really understand the complexity of building hardware, had posted signs on their toolboxes: "Better, Faster, Cheaper. Pick Two.")

On the morning of January 28, 1986, the Space Shuttle, Challenger, blasted off into the unusually cold Florida skies. On board was "America's Teacher in Space," Christa McAuliffe, selected as an astronaut to help captivate an interest in science and engineering among the nation's schoolchildren as well as demonstrate the Shuttle's capability to make spaceflight safe for everyday civilians. It has been estimated that over 17 percent of Americans had tuned in the televisions to watch this historic launch from pad 39B at Florida's Kennedy Space Center.

Within moments, an O-ring joint on the left solid rocket booster began to fail, unleashing a torrent of flame toward the huge main fuel tank next to it. Seconds after Mission Control's command to the astronauts to, "Go with throttle up," Challenger exploded into a huge maelstrom of fire and debris. Seven extraordinary human beings lost their lives that Tuesday morning.

Afterward, the Shuttle program was placed on indefinite hold until the Rodgers Commission, convened at the request of President Reagan, could determine the cause. From a technical standpoint, without a doubt, a poorly designed O-ring joint on the solid booster failed and caused the accident. The faulty design was exacerbated by the freakish cold weather Florida experienced the night before the launch. On that Tuesday morning at Cape Canaveral, the temperature dropped to 24°F, a record that stands to this day. Rubber O-ring material cannot tolerate cold temperatures and becomes much less flexible as its temperature approaches freezing. As Challenger left the pad, the O-ring's pliability was compromised, and the hot exhaust gasses from the solid rocket burned through the O-ring, penetrating the joint and ignited the main fuel tanks filled with highly flammable liquid hydrogen.

But there was a lot more to this tragedy than a simple hardware failure. The root cause to the Shuttle Challenger's loss was traced by the Rodgers Commission to the culture within NASA. Specifically, a managerial pattern of behavior that discouraged and even punished dissenting opinions and made employees feel they were being forced to give their technical consent in order to please management. The Commission blamed NASA's culture by describing the tragedy as, "An accident rooted in history..." and laid responsibility for the loss of crew and vehicle on, "...a decision-making process that led to the launch of Challenger.[5]"

It was found that prior to lift off, numerous engineers had serious reservations about launching Challenger due to the cold weather and the effect it may have on the O-ring joint. NASA management had known for quite a while that the O-ring design was inadequate and presented a potentially catastrophic risk. Shuttle managers actually violated their own rules by launching in weather below 40°F, knowing that at low temperatures, the O-rings would be susceptible to failure. At launch, the Florida sun had barely raised the mercury to 36°F. In the end, NASA managers ignored the advice of engineering to postpone and went ahead with the launch.

As a result of the tragedy, the entire Shuttle Program was grounded for 2.5 years. During this flight suspension, as necessary design changes were made to the Shuttle fleet, NASA agreed to change its management approach, but now under even more public and political pressure to justify the Shuttle program, proceeded with business as usual to get the Shuttle program flying again. Not wanting to look back or even remember the

Figure 1.2 Not how knowledge is shared, or lessons are learned. The Space Shuttle Challenger's debris being loaded into an abandoned missile silo and then entombed with a concrete cover

---

[5] https://science.ksc.nasa.gov/shuttle/missions/51-l/docs/rogers-commission/Chapter-5.txt

tragedy, NASA buried the Challenger artifacts and debris deep within an abandoned missile silo on the Cape Canaveral Air Force Base and then covered it with an immense concrete block.

Seventeen years after the Challenger tragedy, on February 1, 2003, the Space Shuttle Columbia was torn apart over Texas as it came in for re-entry. The technical reason was traced to Columbia's launch when fragments of the foam insulation covering the main fuel tank became dislodged, striking the shuttle's left wing and ripping a large hole into the brittle carbon–carbon material. Upon re-entry into the Earth's atmosphere, superheated plasma formed in the wing's opening causing complete vehicle destruction and the loss of another seven extraordinary human beings.

President George W. Bush appointed the Columbia Accident Investigation Board (CAIB) to determine what caused this tragedy. Again, the Shuttle fleet was to be grounded until the cause was determined and fixed. Again, the CAIB investigators found NASA had much bigger problems than its hardware. NASA's autocratic culture was seen to have never changed—NASA never learned the lessons from the Apollo I fire and the Challenger tragedy. Managers knew on many previous flights that foam was falling off the main tank and was hitting the vehicle, but they continued to fly, despite warnings from engineers.

Afterward, with its aging design and the complexity of operating a vehicle with over one million parts, President Bush called for the eventual ending of the Shuttle program. The CAIB instituted strict new rules for the remaining flights, and NASA management was publicly pilloried.

This time, huge cultural changes were prescribed for NASA. Numerous managers were fired or reassigned and, to guard against another tragedy, NASA introduced an entirely new way to take into account employee feedback in the decision process on all project teams. Called *Technical Authority*, this process ensured that project team engineers having dissenting opinions with their leadership on any technical subject have a path to be heard.

Today, the NASA Knowledge Management office teaches in its courses and case studies that it is not only an obligation that every engineer vocalizes their dissenting opinion but it is every engineers' responsibility, ethically, to state their technical opinion to their management.

If an engineer sees something they are uncomfortable with, whether it be a technical decision made by the project manager or a hardware design they feel is unsafe, they have a process of adjudication to file their dissent. If they cannot come to an understanding with their project manager, an unbiased subject matter expert is brought in to review the complaint. Even at this stage, if the engineer still has reservations, there are formal procedures available where he/she can take it all the way up to the chief engineer and even to Washington, DC and the NASA Administrator.

NASA's new leadership possessed a determination to fundamentally change the agency, and this time, had no intention to simply bury the vehicle wreckage in hopes the tragedy would be forgotten. Instead, the debris from the Space Shuttle Columbia has been preserved and is on display to NASA employees in a special room within the huge Vehicle Assembly Building (VAB), the same facility at the Kennedy Space Center where all shuttles were mated to the fuel tank and external rockets. A visit to this room is similar to attending a wake. You can walk by the landing gear that is still dripping red hydraulic fluid almost two decades later, or the mangled window frames where the astronauts last viewed their home planet before their re-entry, or the countless recognizable portions of the wing and fuselage. You can also see a table holding the personal effects of the astronauts, including a small stuffed doll once given to a crew member by a child and carried aboard for good luck and later recovered in the swampy fields of eastern Texas.

Knowledge management has played an integral part of this new culture and way of doing business at NASA. It was our job, and we had management's full support, to make certain all NASA employees understand their responsibility within the Technical Authority Program. No longer will an engineer feel intimidated or fear reprisal when questioning a technical process or decision. To drive this home, the Knowledge Management Office is located within the Office of the Chief Engineer at Headquarters demonstrating to the entire workforce that upper management at NASA considers training, learning from past mistakes, and Technical Authority as a critical part of their jobs.

The Knowledge Management Office's role in Technical Authority had been threefold. First, we made sure the workforce is aware of the Technical Authority process by the inclusion of Apollo I, Challenger, and Columbia case studies in our coursework. We also promoted it through various videos, podcasts, and a very clearly written description on our website. Second, we helped support the Columbia Room at the VAB where the shuttle debris is stored and placed on display for NASA employees and, third, because not all employees can travel to the Kennedy Space Center to see the Columbia Room, we brought some of the artifacts to each NASA facility across the country and conducted forums about the Columbia Accident.

NASA made a commitment to learn from the mistakes of the past and demonstrated that commitment by transforming an entire agency. Look at what NASA did after the Columbia tragedy—they not only transformed the way they manage projects and their culture, but they published the entire CAIB report detailing the agency's failure during the Columbia mission. What other company or organization is willing to do that? Willing to air their dirty laundry to the entire world? But then, what better way to show your workforce that knowledge management— learning from the past—*and* transparency, is the best way of managing projects and conducting business. Columbia was a horrible tragedy, but NASA learned from it and became a better agency. After all, isn't that what a knowledge management program is supposed to do? Isn't that the real value of lessons learned and knowledge management?

Human spaceflight at NASA carries the most attention and prestige among all the agency's wide portfolio of programs. Mars Rovers, probes traveling to the edge of the solar system, and efficient new jet engines are all incredible feats of engineering, but they are all pieces of metal and electronic componentry. Placing men and women into orbit requires a much higher threshold of safety, reliability, and personal concern. Astronauts are treated special because they are willing to take substantial risks for the advancement of science and engineering and national pride.

Not learning from mistakes can have devastating consequences, not only to an organization, but especially to those employees involved. Bob Ebeling, one of the dissenting engineers who tried to convince his superiors at Morton Thiokol and NASA not to launch the Shuttle Challenger, never got over the tragedy. For the rest of his life, he was haunted by the accident and his role in it. He wondered if he should have tried harder to argue against the launch, perhaps he could have explained his data more clearly or more forcefully. Years later, he told an interviewer, "I think that was one of the mistakes God made. He shouldn't have picked me for that job ... Next time I talk to him, I'm going to ask him, why me? You picked a loser.[6]"

In this chapter, you learned the following:

- The pressure to succeed and meet President Kennedy's mandate to land astronauts on the moon led to very smart and accomplished engineers and managers to make poor decisions. Decisions they later deeply regretted.
- Despite the Apollo 1 disaster, the need to succeed continued to force NASA's management to make risky decisions that eventually led to more catastrophic tragedies.
- It took the death of 17 exceptional human beings before NASA transformed its culture.
- Tragedies such as Apollo 1, Challenger, and Columbia had a personal impact on all the individuals involved in those programs, and the resulting sorrow and guilt last a lifetime.

Questions to consider are given as follows:

- Change is inevitable, and companies and organizations must adapt to these changes in order to be successful. Is your organization's style of management behind the times, perhaps requiring a change in its culture?
- If so, can you visualize how a knowledge management program could assist and support such a change?
- Are budget and/or schedule delays causing managers within your organization to take undue risks?

---

[6] https://nytimes.com/2016/03/26/science/robert-ebeling-challenger-engineer-who-warned-of-disaster-dies-at-89.html

CHAPTER 2

Why Sharing Knowledge Is Critical: Some Historical Perspectives

Stonehenge

About 5,000 years ago, a mysterious tribe of ancient people in the north of Britain began the construction of Stonehenge. This massive project evolved over centuries, as construction was passed on to new groups of nomadic people as they entered and took control of the area. Huge sarsen stones, up to 25 ft. tall and weighing over 30 tons were lugged 18 miles to the site, while other, smaller bluestones weighing between two and five tons were transported from a quarry, an astonishing 150 miles away. These gigantic rocks were then carved and raised vertically to form a circular ring, and then these ancient craftsmen somehow lifted massive slabs atop each vertical pillar.

Why did they build it? Why, over a period of 15 centuries, would a series of different ancient peoples take the time to construct such a massive monument during an epoch where just trying to survive must have been extremely challenging?

How was Stonehenge built? How were those massive stone structures moved over such long distances through marshes and over hills before the invention of the wheel and the introduction of draft animals? How were they chiseled into shape before the Bronze Age and the introduction of metal tools? How were these massive stones raised upright before the invention of the pulley?

We'll never know because, although these highly skilled ancients were believed to be literate, archeologists surmise that the religious beliefs of these prehistoric people prohibited them from recording and writing down their reasons for building Stonehenge and the methods employed to construct it.

Sound outlandishly backward? We can condescendingly view these ancient people as guided by foolish religious rules preventing them from documenting and sharing the knowledge behind their tremendous human achievement. Or we can ask ourselves, how often in today's litigious world does a corporate lawyer recommend that e-mails and other possible documentation and correspondence pertaining to the design, development, and safety testing of a product be deleted or destroyed in order to safeguard the corporation from lawsuits?

The Great Pyramid of Giza

Moving a bit forward, construction of the Great Pyramid was started about 2580 BC, four centuries after construction at Stonehenge had begun. It is the largest of the three pyramids of Giza. With the length of each of its four sides approximately 755 ft. long, the pyramid itself stands at a staggering 481 ft. tall. For over 3,800 years, it stood as the tallest man-made building in the world, only eclipsed when the Lincoln Cathedral's spire was constructed in 1311 in England.

Again, despite the immense efforts to study and understand Egyptian culture and history, we have little idea how these massive pyramids were constructed during an age without iron tools, pulleys, or even wheels. Was this knowledge purposely destroyed, along with many of the slaves who built them, in an effort to protect the Pharaoh and the hidden treasures buried within them? Or, as many modern Egyptologists speculate, did knowledge of building these monumental tombs simply die out over time and evaporate because there was no longer a need for building more pyramids?

Organizations risk losing critical knowledge the same way the ancient Egyptians lost their ability to build pyramids. This can happen when critical knowledge is undocumented or when a highly skilled (i.e., knowledgeable) employee jumps to a competitor or simply decides to retire, taking that critical knowledge with him/her. Today, most programs and projects are certainly documented, but there's still a chance of losing critical knowledge and then trying to relearn this hard-earned knowledge.

The Black Death

During the 14th century, the Black Death killed between a third and a half of the population of Europe. This horrific pandemic peaked between 1347 and 1351 but also returned, just when a weary population thought it was finally over, in several new, deadly waves for decades afterward. In 1346, the population of Europe was approximately 150 million. By 1353, only seven years later, the population was 70 to 75 million. It took almost 300 years for Europe to recover to its pre-plague numbers.

Unfortunately, in those days, only 10 to 15 percent of the population was literate, and many of those who could read and write were lost to the plague, so it's almost impossible to fully understand how such a calamitous pandemic started and spread so quickly because so few were able to chronicle the nightmare. Certainly, to those who endured and suffered through it, it must have seemed like the end of times.

Today, everyone may be literate to varying degrees, but we still lose the lessons of the past because we don't take the time to document them. Maybe we're too busy or maybe we just don't like writing. Or maybe we just don't care, so we "kick the can down the road" and figure those in the future who encounter the same issues will just have to figure it out on their own. If you're a responsible manager wanting to see your organization succeed, even after you've left, you'll realize how important it will be moving forward to understand the problems faced in the past.

During the Black Death, Europe possessed a highly specialized economy ruled by guilds designed to keep exclusive control of their trades by keeping strict limits on their numbers and preventing the tricks of their trades from being shared. When the plague raged through medieval towns and cities, it ravaged these concentrated groups of tradespeople along with their specialized knowledge. An entire region or country could find itself not only without the services of a tailor, a carpenter, a shoemaker, or a wool spinner, but also the very knowledge how to do those trades. When the plague relented, these skills had to be relearned all over again.

How often do modern organizations go to extreme lengths to protect their knowledge? Lessons learned databases may exist, but they're hidden behind firewalls where only a select few can actually access and learn from them. Companies attempt to classify almost everything they develop, even simple Excel spreadsheet macros, as proprietary information or tools and limit access because of concerns an employee may walk away with corporate secrets. But, at the same time, they are hoping to protect internal knowledge, they are also risking that it will never be appropriately shared with those who need it.

Roman Cement

Today, almost 2,000 years later, we can still see and experience the power and the extent of Roman culture through the countless ancient buildings, aqueducts, and bridges still standing as a memorial to Roman ingenuity and prowess. The reason the Roman Coliseum still stands and captivates tourists is that it was, like most of the Roman structures, built with a cement that had the remarkable ability to withstand thermal expansion without cracking or deteriorating. With the fall of Rome, this unique cement recipe was lost. Although modern Portland cement surpasses the cement the Romans invented in compressive strength, it has never been able to match ancient Roman cement in withstanding the effects of weathering. One just needs to see how modern bridges and infrastructures tend to need considerable maintenance after only several decades of weathering. Compare that to the Coliseum in Rome.

Medieval Monks

But, before we end our brief history lesson involving knowledge management, let's consider a success story. In the late 500s, the once all-powerful Roman Empire was disintegrating, and the European continent found itself at the mercy of roaming bands of barbarian armies intent on destroying everything that represented Greco-Roman culture that had pervaded Europe during the past 1,000 years. Chaos and fear reigned for a century as all components of civilization—cities, commerce, farming, churches, schools, libraries, and public infrastructures were reduced to rubble and the real Dark Ages descended upon Europe.

What we now call *Western Civilization* would have been eradicated, had it not been for the vigilance and foresight of medieval monks. Behind the protective stone walls of monasteries all across Europe, monks copied thousands of Greek and Roman manuscripts saving the works of such ancient philosophers as Aristotle and Plato, Cicero and Seneca, and countless others whose thoughts and writings enabled the future development of such institutions as democracy, freedom of thought and expression, and the legal rights of an individual in his/her pursuit of happiness. The monks' tenacity protected and preserved the very knowledge that would eventually lift Europe from the Dark Ages to the Renaissance and later, the Enlightenment. Western man wasn't forced to learn this knowledge all over again, the conscientious brothers of Benedictine and countless other monasteries scattered throughout the European countryside saved these priceless books and knowledge from which we benefit, even today.

History often reminds us, we aren't smarter than our ancient ancestors. They had exactly the same brain capacity or ability to comprehend and understand as we do, today. Our advantage is our knowledge, our ability to learn from the past. We learn from the mistakes and successes of those who went before us. We're not smarter or more clever than our ancient ancestors; we simply have the advantage of hindsight and the advantage, if we take it, of learning from their mistakes.

And, a final observation, knowledge management shouldn't be seen as an activity reserved exclusively for organizations and corporations hoping to improve productivity and efficiency by learning from the past. On a more intimate level, we can also gain the benefits of knowledge management in our personal lives. As a parent, did you ever wish you had the opportunity to ask your deceased mother how she coped with misbehaving toddlers or uncommunicative teenagers? Did you ever wish you could have one last conversation with a grandparent to discover what it was like growing up in a foreign land and all the hardships they struggled with in order to build a better life for all? Don't you wish you could share their story and the lessons they learned during their life's journey with your own children? Or perhaps you remember that your father used to have leg problems that now, 40 years later, are plaguing you. Wouldn't it be helpful to be able to ask him, what he did to solve the leg spasms that are now torturing you? The goal of knowledge management is to gather and share this kind of critical knowledge, too. Now is the time to manage and share it, before it's too late.

Let's move on from the Druids of ancient Britain, the Pharaohs of Egypt, and the devastation of the Black Death and look at ways knowledge management and sharing can provide a very practical and substantial benefit within our modern organizations.

In this chapter, you learned the following:

- History shows that when programs and projects begin, knowledge management is rarely considered.
- Losing critical knowledge is not new, and its consequences can be profound.
- Knowledge sharing can also be a beneficial part of our personal lives.

Questions to consider are as follows:

- How were the knowledge and lessons learned captured on projects you have been involved with in the past?
- Can you recall any specific problems or difficulties that were solved previously but never captured and, subsequently, had to be learned all over, again?
- How much effort and cost does it take to record knowledge and lessons learned compared to the cost of relearning them?

CHAPTER 3

What Is Lean Knowledge Management?

The key to lean knowledge management (Lean KM) is determining who your audience is and what knowledge they need to successfully complete their jobs. Lean KM involves gathering and sharing only the pertinent knowledge that helps them do their work safely, effectively, and efficiently. In other words, it's getting critical knowledge to the folks in your organization who need it the most. It requires filtering and scrubbing out anything that may be considered superfluous or inapplicable to your defined audience. It involves getting crucial information to the crucial people in your organization.

It's described as *lean* because it is focused only on the specific knowledge that needs to be gathered and shared with the defined audience. It purposely leaves out types of knowledge that are peripheral or irrelevant to your defined audience. By being *lean*, it allows an organization to quickly gather and disseminate crucial information to the people who need it most.

Important Lean KM Definitions

Before proceeding further, we need to define a few terms relating to lean KM:

- Customers/audience: The group of people within an organization who will benefit the most from the knowledge you share. This is the group that needs KM the most. *Audience* and *customers* are two words that will be interchangeable throughout this book. When considering your customers, always ask, "What do you need?"

- Knowledge: Critical information that can be embodied in lessons learned, case studies, advice, know-how, training courses, and best practices that can make your customer's job easier or more efficient or more productive.
- KM: Consists of three primary phases:
  - Gathering: Discovering where potential pockets of knowledge may be located, or even hidden, within your organization.
  - Filtering: Determining which components of the knowledge you have gathered is usable and helpful to your customers. Think of it this way: there's tons of *information* out there, but it doesn't become *knowledge* until you filter out the components that your customers need to successfully do their jobs.
  - Sharing: Finding the most effective way to disseminate this knowledge to your customers.
- Stakeholders: The group in an organization that supports your lean KM efforts because they believe in the value of KM. Stakeholders are typically members of management who acknowledge that KM can help an organization become more efficient and more productive. Most importantly, stakeholders set the tone, let you know what areas within the organization need help. Most importantly, stakeholders possess the funding, the ultimate power. If they see your KM program will bring value to their organization, you will gain their support, if not... When considering your stakeholders, always ask, "How can I be of help?"
- Champion: This is the person in your organization, usually in upper management, who understands the benefits of KM and is willing to use his/her influence and power to get a program in place. Without a champion's support, you may have a very tough road ahead. A champion is willing to accept a bit of risk because your success or failure will be a reflection on their career as well as yours. When dealing with your KM champion, always keep them in the loop and make them aware of all you've accomplished.

Lean KM Versus Traditional KM Programs

So, why *lean KM*? Because it's the simplest and most effective way to transfer knowledge, and it's the easiest KM effort to sell to your stakeholders. KM doesn't need to be so complicated. Lean KM strips away all the confusing terms that only academics and high-priced consultants understand, it filters out all the noise, and all the information, data, and knowledge that is not immediately pertinent to your workforce/audience/customers.

When looking for the funding to start a KM program, it's a lot easier to approach your stakeholders by describing a program that is solely devoted to improving their workforce's efficiency and effectiveness than approaching them with a more typical KM project plan containing complex and almost indecipherable terminology usually accompanied by indefensible funding requests.

There's nothing wrong with the more traditional KM programs taught in academia. As a matter of fact, they conduct some excellent research in the field of knowledge and keep the KM topic fresh and resilient. But lean KM recognizes that your stakeholders, and particularly your customers, may not be interested in the broad field of KM, they just want the results of all that work done in academia, and they just want a tool to make their jobs easier.

KM doesn't need to be complicated. As a matter of fact, you begin to lose customers and your entire *raison d'être* when things become overly complicated. And, once you lose customers, your stakeholders will soon follow. Your customers, the organization's workforce, aren't interested in the theory of knowledge, or pedagogy or taxonomy, they're interested in solving their problems. The job of lean KM is simple and should not be complicated by information and terminology your customers may find confusing. In a nutshell, lean KM researches how difficulties and problems were dealt with in the past and then gets that information to your workforce as quickly and concisely as possible.

Too often, KM programs never get off the ground because they are unable to explain to their stakeholders exactly how they're going to help the organization, or fail soon after the start, because they haven't defined their customers and then don't understand how to deal with, or filter, the mountains of information out there into something useful for their customers.

Lean Knowledge Management: Origins From the Past

Lean KM and attempting to gather critical knowledge and get it to the people who need it most isn't a new concept. Diderot, the French philosopher during the Enlightenment, conducted the first attempt to gather and catalog all the *useful* knowledge of his age into one, concise book, the *Encyclopédie*. From Diderot's standpoint, the clergy, aristocrats, and scholars of his era understood history, mathematics, science, and the laws of physics, but the general population didn't understand the more pragmatic, the more useful knowledge concerning how things actually worked and how men and women working in the various trades make and manufacture the growing number of products that society was becoming dependent upon. Diderot defined his audience, not as the upper class of his day, but rather the bourgeoisie, the middle class, and wanted to accumulate and share all the practical, useful knowledge with them and ensure this knowledge was passed down to future generations. An educated scholar of the Enlightenment might understand the earth's orbit around the sun and even such cosmic events as solar eclipses and the moon's effect on tides, but Diderot wanted to document not only this esoteric knowledge but also the practical knowledge of the age and share it with everyone. How a shoemaker tanned leather and shaped it to make shoes, or how the baker selected ingredients, kneaded dough, and baked bread, or the secret process a vintner used to ferment wine.

Diderot was doing exactly what we are trying to accomplish with lean KM by defining his audience (for Diderot, the bourgeoisie), and then gathering and syphoning information into useful knowledge. To Diderot, the world had spent too much time and effort concentrating on religious debates and the history of kings and wars; now it was time to concentrate on the more practical and useful components of our lives—the mechanical arts and the knowledge that make this new world work. Diderot's *Encyclopédie* was the Wikipedia and Google of its time, and his efforts at consolidating useful information into genuine knowledge helped spur the Industrial Revolution.

So, how do you determine knowledge for your customers?
In this chapter, you learned the following:

- Lean KM is different from the traditional or academic KM approach. Lean is designed specifically (and unconditionally) to be a practical benefit that helps your workforce do their jobs as effectively as possible. It is a simple and cost-effective way to help your organization be successful.
- The essential first step to lean KM is defining your audience.
- There's a significant difference between *information* and *knowledge*. Information is everywhere and is basically useless to your workforce until it is refined into the knowledge they need to be successful.
- For lean KM to work, you not only need to define your audience but you also need to determine your stakeholders and, hopefully, discover a champion who will support KM.
- Lean KM means defining your audience, refining information into knowledge, sharing this knowledge with the people who need it most.

Questions to consider are as follows:

- What group within your organization would you define as your KM audience?
- Would providing a robust lean KM program to this group help your organization's ability to be successful?
- Is information simply considered the same thing as knowledge in your organization? Or is it filtered into the knowledge and then shared with those people within your organization who have the biggest impact on profit?
- Can you identify a KM champion within your organization?

CHAPTER 4

Essential Steps to Implement a Knowledge Management Program in Your Organization

Define Your Audience to Discover What Type of Knowledge to Gather

As a knowledge manager, it's your job to define your audience—those who will have the greatest impact on your organization's success. What is their primary mission? Health care? Manufacturing? Engineering design? Training? You need to determine this so that you can focus on the type of knowledge they need. At NASA, our focus was on the technical workforce, the men and women working on project teams that develop space and aeronautics hardware, and the new technologies that enable advancements in science and engineering.

Once you define your audience, you will know what type of knowledge you need to gather—the knowledge available to make their jobs more productive, safer, and more efficient.

As mentioned in Chapter 4, unless you place boundaries on what you consider knowledge, you'll be overwhelmed trying to manage it. After all, almost everything can be considered knowledge, if you allow it. Let's say you're a jet engine manufacturer trying to develop a knowledge management (KM) plan. Unless you draw limits, things like the blueprints for the building you're in, the enormous IT infrastructure, the instruction manuals for the plant machinery, or even the user's manual for the microwave oven in the employee cafeteria can be seen as *knowledge* for someone in the organization. Unless you define audience/customers and limit yourself to gathering the knowledge they need, you will be enduring an unending process of categorizing information that no one needs and no one will ever use. KM can include everything, if you allow it, but then it ends up being nothing much useful to anybody.

Be prepared to fend off others. Numerous times, other organizational entities within NASA wanted to be included in our KM program. IT folks, in particular, thought that their task to understand and catalog all of NASA's IT infrastructure, including every website, electronic subscription, piece of software, virus and spam control, and so on, should be part of the agency's overall KM program. Certainly, this is important information, but it applies specifically to the IT and networking divisions within NASA and was unneeded information for our customers—engineers, technicians, and researchers.

Our audience, the technical workforce, the engineers designing flight hardware, the engineering managers trying to understand and evaluate complex systems, and technicians assembling probes to travel throughout the solar system aren't particularly concerned about lessons learned from the IT operations unit. Certainly, these organizations need KM, but their work and their audience are so specialized that they need their own specific KM program. If someone comes toward you talking about incorporating Big Data into your KM program, your best response might be to help them develop their own lean IT KM program that is specific to their own needs.

In the past, I was asked if we'd accept lessons learned or case studies from secretaries and administrative personnel, procurement specialists, and legislative affairs officers. Again, certainly their jobs were important, and certainly, they had valuable advice to share with others in their respective organizations, but if I broadened our scope beyond the technical workforce, I would have never been able to get a handle on such a mountain of information and, as a result, my real audience, the technical workforce, would suffer.

At NASA, almost every center had an old-fashioned research library containing thousands of books and technical papers. Well, what could be defined more as *knowledge* than a library? And frequently we were asked, why don't we place the responsibility (and the costs) of these libraries under KM? Libraries can be great resources, but research libraries may be a bit outdated in our Internet age. Libraries are also very expensive, and they serve a very limited customer base, in this case, mostly research scientists. I understood the importance of traditional libraries but felt they were mostly a peripheral resource for my KM customers. Engineers and technicians on project teams seldom look for information about their jobs at a library. Again, if I had consented, my customers were the ones who would have suffered. One thing you should be careful of is other internal organizations, particularly ones with declining budgets, looking to utilize your budget in the name of KM.

Now that you have defined your audience and know what type of knowledge they need to do their jobs effectively, you need to convince your management of the importance of KM and especially how a vibrant, lean KM program can help *them*. As every project manager knows, one of the cardinal rules for successful projects is gaining upper management's support. Without this, you'll find yourself on a nearly impossible task headed for certain doom.

Define Your Stakeholders and Gain Their Support

There are two groups you always need to be aware of, the first was discussed previously, your customers, the second group you need to always be mindful of are your stakeholders. Your stakeholders are the people in upper management who understand the value of KM and are willing to support it. They hold the power and funding to help you design and build a successful program.

At first, you may need to convince potential stakeholders about the benefits and values of a vibrant KM program and, even after gaining that initial support, you will need to follow up with your stakeholders to demonstrate your KM success and accomplishments.

It's not easy proposing a new KM program that can seldom show tangible, quantifiable results proving it is saving the company money and helping it make a profit. So, how do you convince a management whose main concern, rightfully so, is protecting the bottom line? Well, here are some pointers to consider when trying to convince potential stakeholders about the promise of KM:

- KM has two fundamental components: gathering knowledge and sharing this knowledge. The function of sharing knowledge with the workforce is a facet of training, and everyone knows training (or sharing knowledge) is going to help a workforce maintain its effectiveness. If you're dealing strictly with a bean counter mentality in your organization, you'll never be able to prove that training saved your organization a specific amount of money as a return on investment, there's no getting around this, it's simply unquantifiable. But, you can change the debate from *return on investment* to *return on mission success*. You can determine the value of KM when it is seen as a tool for mission success, whether that mission involves building a rocket, processing banking transactions, manufacturing widgets, customer service, or patient care. You can substantiate positive *returns on mission success* by gathering pertinent metrics from your customers from postevent questionnaires asking participants to describe what they learned from attending a course or KM function or, taking it a step further, interviewing their managers to inquire if they've noticed an improvement after an employee utilized your KM resources.

- Within your organization, knowledge is free, it's an incredible value-added component of your operations. Critical knowledge is sitting out there waiting to be gathered, processed, and shared. But this valuable knowledge is being retained by people who can retire or leave your organization at a moment's notice. This corporate knowledge won't be out there for long, and once it's gone, it can become very expensive for an organization to relearn these lost assets. Skills, knowledge, and lessons that are currently free could instantly become very expensive. There are already numerous people within your organization who have specific knowledge and insight how to do complex tasks that result in your company operating successfully. These critical players are already on your payroll and their knowledge and wisdom is right there, ready for the picking. Your company already *owns* the critical knowledge these people possess. But, unless this free knowledge, this hidden asset, is managed (gathered, processed, and shared), it can be lost, for example, when a crucial person retires. Once this happens and the organization realizes the impact, it becomes very expensive to go out and hire consultants to come in and show you how you used to do things successfully. I once had a very frank conversation with a manager from an aerospace company that made jet engines. I asked what they do when critical folks retire? What is your company's succession plan? The response was typical for most organizations: "We end up hiring them back as consultants for two or three times their previous salary."

- How costly is it for your company to make the same mistake, twice? How often is the same mistake made over and over? Remind your management of the Brazilian novelist, Paulo Coelho, who once wrote: "A mistake repeated more than once is a decision." The whole idea of lessons learned and KM is to learn from the past in order to prevent the same mistakes from impacting production and profit. Lean KM can be a sure pathway to more effective and efficient operations.

- When selling a KM program to upper management within a corporation or industry, it is critical to stress the cost savings that sharing critical knowledge can attain and how it can affect the bottom line. After all, mistakes and rework always come with a price tag. When selling a KM program to a government agency, it may be more important to stress the agency's perception in the eyes of the tax paying public. Governmental failures often lead to well-publicized public inquiries featuring a host of participants anxious to destroy an agency's reputation or an employee's career. In the Beltway area of DC, it's called passing the Washington Post front page test. No one in government wants their agency's mistakes headlining the Washington Post. A KM program can help ensure your agency passes the test.

- KM not only can help stabilize the bottom line and increase profits, but it can also enhance an organization's reputation with its customers. In an incredibly competitive marketplace, today's consumers have little tolerance for poorly designed or manufactured products. In reality, a company is seldom given a second chance by a consumer after feeling burned by a less than adequate product. Ever feel like you got mislead or cheated by an automaker after purchasing a lemon? What are the chances your next car will be the same brand? A strong KM program can help stop that lemon leaving the shop floor.

- A vibrant KM program can build a stronger corporate culture by engaging employees and letting them know how important they are and how critical the work they do is for the success of the organization. KM can boost the morale of a workforce by reaching out and asking for their help in developing a working environment that values their input. At NASA, we actively sought to get employees to contribute to the lessons learned database, to write articles and case studies to be published on our website, or to feel comfortable discussing problems they encountered while participating in our courses and forums. This made employees feel as if they were part of our KM program, and they were part of helping NASA become a better agency.

- As with most organizations, the people at the top, those making the decisions, aren't always privy to this incredibly crucial knowledge that resides on the shop floor, the hospital floor, or within the sales force. KM can be a way of directly communicating potential problems or opportunities from the workforce to the executive suites. Managers need to know data and information in order to make the proper decision. A well-designed KM program can do this. As an example, at NASA, we conducted a monthly review of searches made within our lessons learned database and deliver the top 10 searched for topics to the agency's chief engineer in order to give a heads-up on what potential problems the workforce appears to be encountering.

- Leadership programs within your organization should be exposed to your KM efforts. KM is, in a very real sense, a history of your organization that provides insights as to what worked and didn't work, what helped, and what hurt the company in the past. It's a perfect opportunity to make sure the folks being developed to become new institutional leaders experience the value of KM.

- Ask your stakeholders what kind of culture do you want to build within your organization? One of punishing mistakes in order to prevent them or one of learning from mistakes so that they won't happen again? A culture based on sharing lessons learned is not looking to blame anyone, it is looking to fix a broken process so that it won't happen again. It's looking to save your organization money by preventing accidents and costly mistakes.

- In the workplace, very few people look forward to change. Using case studies that demonstrate that change is inevitable and, if done right, can have a successful outcome for all. KM can partner with change management to help an organization adapt to change.

- Finally, keep this gem of a quote handy when preparing a presentation to management for KM buy-in: "An investment in knowledge always pays the best interest." Everyone respects the timeless wisdom of Ben Franklin.

Remember, when proposing to management the implementation of a lean KM program, avoid purely academic descriptions of the theory of knowledge, taxonomy, and so on and, instead, focus on the practical aspects noted earlier—basically, it can prevent mistakes and save money. What rational person can turn down a proposal that promises that?

KM is free. It's out there for the grabbing. There is no way KM can hurt your operations, it can only help. You can lose critical information that effects the entire operation in a heartbeat if you don't act quickly. What happens when you lose this critical knowledge? You can only get it back two ways, and neither is preferable. You can make the same mistake twice and finally learn from it, or you can go out and hire very expensive consultants to give you back the knowledge you once possessed for free. As Sir Francis Bacon, the English philosopher who has been credited with developing the scientific method, once wrote, "Knowledge is power." Harness the power or ignore it at your own risk.

The Knowledge Chain of Command

You've defined your audience, you've defined what type of knowledge you need to manage for this audience, you've convinced management of the benefits of your program; now, before you can develop a KM plan, you need to specify how you will be the intermediary between your KM operations and your management chain of command. Who should you report to? Ideally, this should be a two-way street, where you can deliver information and potential problems to a manager who needs this feedback and is also willing to use your KM program to share his/her ideas and concerns to the workforce.

Again, the first step is to define who in the management chain within your organization will be the primary beneficiary of your KM program. What person, or group of persons, will find the knowledge you gather to be influential in his/her decision-making process? The chief knowledge officer (CKO) needs to report directly to the person in an organization with responsibility for making decisions that affect your customers—your organization's workforce. For example, at NASA, our customers were the technical workforce, so it made sense that the CKO reported directly to the chief engineer.

And, importantly, at NASA, the CKO was classified as an *advisor* and did not have any role in decision making other than giving correct and useful data to the chief engineer. Because the CKO reported directly, and only to the chief engineer, no one could supersede or influence what information is passed on to the chief engineer. The CKO had the ear of the chief engineer.

And, finally, when speaking of an organization's chain of command and stakeholders, share in your KM success. Let your stakeholders and, in particular, your champions get the credit they deserve because without them, you wouldn't have the support needed for a successful program.

In this chapter, you learned the following:

- For NASA, we defined our audience as the technical workforce, those men and women involved in designing, fabricating, and assembling aerospace hardware.
- Although NASA has many more departments and units supporting its mission, we concentrate only on the technical workforce, those who have the biggest impact on NASA's success.
- You have defined your audience and, hopefully, a champion willing to support your effort. Now you need to convince your organization's management of the importance of a robust lean KM program and how it can help them.
- Lean KM is much more than cataloging lessons learned. It is designed specifically to improve your organization's bottom line.
- You won't be able to quantify the return on investment a lean KM program may generate, but you can demonstrate its impact on the return on mission success.
- Critical knowledge is free, but if you lose it, reacquiring it can be very costly.
- Lean KM can be a venue where upper management can communicate directly with the workforce. This can develop into a more inclusive corporate culture where the workforce feels respected while engaged with their management.
- NASA is an engineering and science organization, and to emphasize upper management's support for KM, it was placed under the leadership of the Office of the Chief Engineer.

Questions to consider are as follows:

- You know your stakeholders, your management, how receptive are they to supporting a lean KM program.
- Can you explain (and sell) the differences between lean KM and the more traditional KM programs that may have been tried in the past?
- Can you recall any instance within your organization where critical knowledge was lost? Where the same mistake happened over and over, again?
- Within your corporate structure, where would a KM office best be placed to demonstrate management's support?

CHAPTER 5

Developing a KM Program Office

With your plan in place, upper management's support, and your customers defined, you need to carefully develop an effective structure for your knowledge management program office. It's critical that your office's function is well defined and tightly organized because you have a large task in front of you. You're going to gather, process, and share knowledge, and you're going to need to develop a set of metrics that will provide justification for your efforts.

To be successful, it is essential to follow standardized project management procedures. It is beyond the scope of this book to describe in detail how to design and develop an appropriate project management office, but you can start off with clearly established lines of authority and responsibility within your office so that everyone fully understands their roles and also understands they will be held responsible for performing those roles. Don't allow any overlap of responsibilities between team members and make sure to define each person's role as clearly as possible.

KM Program Management Office

A good program management structure won't help much unless you recruit good people. Good people, though, come at a premium, so don't be surprised if other departments within your organization fight to retain the people you have your eye on. Too often, in a production environment, activities such as KM are seen as subordinate to operations. Many managers may believe KM is important, but not more important than getting product out the door. You need to remind everyone that your KM program is a critical component to ensuring good product goes out the door. If you ask departments to volunteer folks for your KM program, don't be surprised if you end up with the people they're trying to get rid of. Again, the importance of explaining the value of KM to your stakeholders may have a huge impact on gaining the best people for your team.

Before discussing how to construct a KM program for your organization, it's important to briefly consider the value of having sound customer service. You always want to be seen within your organization as a professional operation, and it starts with customer service. Whatever types of knowledge sharing events you host (we'll focus on the various types in Chapter 6), you want to make certain those attending feel they were treated respectfully and courteously through the entire event process. Communicate directly with your customers to make sure they know where meetings, forums, or courses are to be held, and make sure they are aware of any prereading materials. Having a staff trained to pay attention to the little things, such as being prompt in returning calls and e-mails, politely listening and responding to comments and suggestions, pays large dividends in the future. You can inadvertently spoil a learning event for a customer by inattentive or rude treatment, but you can also get your customer on your side early by treating them with the courtesy and respect they deserve. Strong customer service from your Program Management Office (PMO) will also demonstrate strong management and leadership skills to your stakeholders. Have you ever found yourself really looking forward to dinner out at a new restaurant only to have it spoiled because of bad service? Usually, when that happens, you never go back to that restaurant despite the fact they may have a delicious menu. Customer service is critical.

Once your event has finished, you're going to want customer feedback concerning not only the event itself and whether they gained value from it, but also feedback on how they felt they were treated and kept informed by your personnel. When reporting metrics to your stakeholders, positive customer feedback can be a very powerful message coming directly from the workforce.

When reviewing customer feedback, be cognizant that some people are never going to be happy. The room was too cold, too hot, the coffee was a brand they didn't like, the chairs were uncomfortable, and so on. Listen, be attentive, and courteous, but you need to filter out the noise and concentrate on real, genuine constructive criticism concerning issues that you can control and improve.

In designing your knowledge management program, you want to make sure lines of communication are streamlined as efficiently as possible. You need to select various lead managers and divide areas of responsibility among them. By doing so, you are consciously delegating your authority and trust to your team leads to get their jobs done, and you are now performing the project manager role as an organizer, leader, facilitator, and coach.

At NASA, because we combined our training program with knowledge management, we created the following KM program management structure, as depicted in Figure 5.1:

We will refer back to integrating training with knowledge later, but for now, notice the strategy in our KM program structure. We broke up the four main functions of our office: leadership training, knowledge management, project management office, and training with each being headed by a lead person responsible for the operations listed as follows:

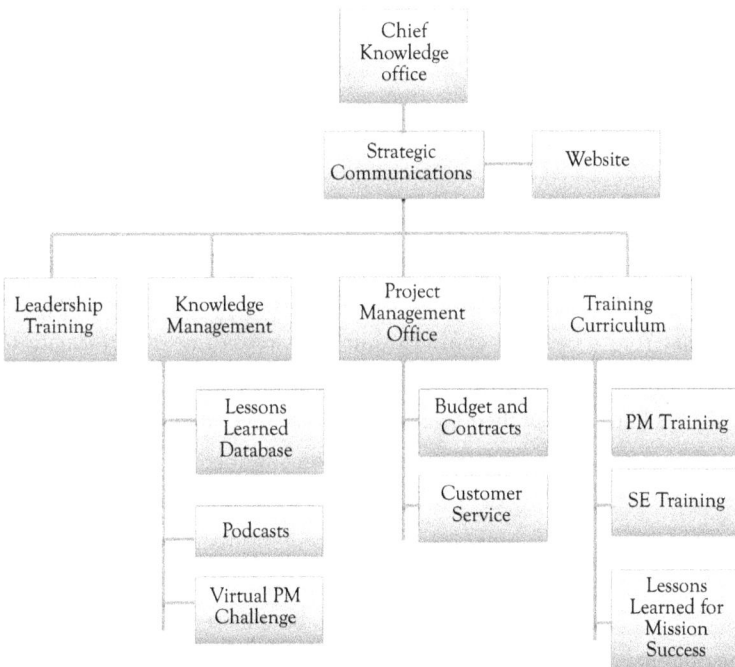

Figure 5.1 KM program management structure

Sharing knowledge was our most critical task, whether it be through a lessons learned database, case studies, forums or coursework, so we placed the strategic communications function between the Chief Knowledge Officer (CKO) and the rest of the team. This ensured that the strategic communications component was aware of all work done by the team and was responsible for disseminating their efforts with our workforce. In a world where knowledge must eventually be digitized in order to share it, the strategic communications function must be a focal point of all activities.

The most effective way to keep our NASA customers informed was through our website. We spent a lot of time and effort making sure this website could function as a *one-stop shop* for any engineer or technician serving on a project team to find whatever information they might need: career resources such as a competency models to review and determine their weaknesses and strengths, a course catalog to select training for career growth, a searchable knowledge inventory to locate lessons learned, video interviews, leadership program content, podcasts, and case studies.

The website has to be designed with simplicity and rigor because it is your most effective tool to share knowledge with your customers who are already very busy on their jobs and need information as quickly and con-cisely as possible. At NASA, our customers were engineers, technicians, and scientists tasked with designing and building one-of-a-kind hardware that was always on the cutting edge of current technologies. These men and women have very stressful and busy jobs, and they have little time or patience for overly ornate or cluttered websites when searching for answers. Your customers come to your KM website to get information, not to suffer through gimmicky web design features. Too often, website designers like to show their creativity and become infatuated with elabo-rate features and tools that may be useful on commercial sites, but are lit-tle more than annoying on a website whose purpose is pure functionality.

Within our KM program was the project management office, or PMO as it is usually referred to. The function of the PMO was to estab-lish processes and procedures that must be adhered to by each team member in order to establish a set of standard operating procedures. Our PMO designed the process of using *concept documents* to track each task. For example, if we were designing a new course, the person responsible for working with subject matter experts and course design experts would write up a concept document describing the task, duration, estimated cost, and deliverables. The person assigned to manage this task would be required to update it weekly with progress reports in our online database. The concept document would be color-coded green—all good, yellow—having some concerns, and red—we got problems. Every two weeks, I'd call a team meeting, and we'd go through the status of each concept document. I found these team meetings to be helpful in a number of ways. Obviously, a face-to-face status report where we openly discuss problems and issues as a group is always helpful, but it also allows everyone to participate in suggestions and problem-solving for each task as team. At NASA, these meetings were almost like team-building exercises because within the KM program, I wanted to be inclusive and ensure transparency in everything our team did, and by openly discussing each task's difficulties and opportunities with the entire team, it enabled an environment of openness as well as a feeling of team membership.

In order to keep a database, not only of all the concept documents but also the myriad amount of information and documentation a project team needs at a quick notice, it's extremely helpful to utilize an internal webbased application allowing the team to catalog and share these resources. There are a wide variety of these applications readily available at reasonable costs. Having everything online makes documents, updates, and communications easily accessible and keeps the entire team on the same page.

This isn't the place to delve deep into the subject of project management. There are a lot of good books and courses available, but I would think, in most cases, your KM program is going to be on a much smaller scale than the typical projects within your organization that need to develop very involved and somewhat complicated project management structures. But, here's a list of essentials needed to run an efficient knowledge management program:

- Write a project plan. This will clearly define your customers and keep your team focused on their job of gathering the knowledge your customers need to be successful. A clearly, well-defined project plan is essential to minimize any requirement and scope creep that almost always seems to happen with ill-defined or nonexistent project plans. The project plan will also include a description of the various ways your team will gather and share knowledge with the workforce.

- Your project plan is also the most important document you will deliver to your stakeholders. Clearly state your objectives, scope, and resources you will need. Make it as clear, concise, and as simple as possible.

- Be honest about your funding requirements. New projects with high price tags come under a great deal of scrutiny.

- Understand your role as a project manager. You're a manager and leader, and your role is to determine strategy and guide your team by running interference, clearing the way and facilitating their work. You need to understand what each team member's tasks involve, and you need to monitor their progress and get resources to help them if progress isn't being made. For some, because knowledge management can be very interesting work, it can be tempting to slowly immerse themselves into the details of each task and suddenly discover they are micromanaging their team. A good project manager knows how to delegate.

- Once you're up and running, you need to track your team's progress by developing the right type of metrics. You need metrics that mean something, especially to your stakeholders. You need to select the right set of metrics so that someone can see at one glance your progress.

- Utilize your metrics to keep everyone informed. Transparency is the best policy, let your customers and stakeholder become aware of your successes and, also, areas that may require improvement.

- You need to develop consistent internal processes that aren't put in place to create busy work, but rather provide standardized, logical procedures that everyone on the team follows. For example, every Friday by close of business every team member must have their concept document status updated so that you, as the program manager, can be prepared on Monday morning to address any issues.

- Document internal processes—this is knowledge management, after all. Your internal processes may become critical knowledge that you need to some day pass on to your successor or to other organizations hoping to develop a KM program. An example of an internal process would be designing a template for standardizing the development of knowledge sharing events. Document the various steps and gates required along the design path such as, reaching out to subject matter experts, locating instructors or facilitators, gathering a review team, presenting a pilot, and then reviewing evaluations and, finally, holding a lessons learned meeting.

A Federated Approach to KM

Most large organizations have numerous product lines. Corporations such as General Electric, for example, produce a wide variety of products such as train locomotives, refrigerators, jet engines and financial services, just to name a few. If you have a large organization with diverse work products, you may want to adopt a federated approach to knowledge management. This system allows you to appoint a chief knowledge officer for each product area of your organization. The lessons learned from manufacturing locomotives might not always apply to the folks in your organization doing financial transactions.

Under a federated approach, each product line maintains their own KM program because they know their areas of expertise better than anyone else. This doesn't mean sharing of knowledge between these different product lines doesn't take place. We developed a federated system of KM at NASA that allows each of NASA's 10 centers to appoint their own chief knowledge officer. Each NASA center had their own field of aerospace expertise, so it makes sense that they should manage their own knowledge. But this doesn't mean the centers don't share where applicable. All agency CKOs met regularly as a group to look for areas of collaboration and share efforts that may be mutually beneficial.

In this chapter, you learned the following:

- Your lean KM project needs to be managed with traditional, proven project management rigor and procedures.
- When designing your KM office, clearly mark areas of responsibility and hold team members accountable.
- Your website is your most critical avenue of communications with your audience/customers. Make it simple and easy to use and find critical knowledge. If your customers find it difficult or confusing to use, they may not be back.
- You need to ensure your staff concentrates on exceptional customer service. Your defined audience is also your customers, and they represent the only reason your KM office is in existence. You serve your customers.

Questions to consider are as follows:

- Do you have the necessary project management experience to set up a lean KM program? If not, do you have access to training or other resources to develop these skills?
- NASA is a large organization with a diversified portfolio of programs and projects. Because of this, it was decided agencywide KM would be better served with a de-centralized model. What would work best for your organization?

CHAPTER 6

Gathering and Sharing Knowledge

As mentioned earlier, there's a lot of *information* out there that needs to be filtered and refined before it becomes the *knowledge* your workforce needs. And now, once you have the knowledge you want to share with your customers, you need to find the most efficient and effective route to get this information to the people who need it most. But first, it's critical to place high standards on your efforts to filter information into useful knowledge.

Filtering the Right Information

The 18th century writer, philosopher and historian, Voltaire, once wrote, "History is a pack of lies!" and Winston Churchill, the British prime minister during the Second World War as well as a gifted historian once said, "History is written by the victors!"

What does history have to do with knowledge management? Well, the whole reason for studying history is to learn from the past to make sure you don't repeat the same mistake. To repeat the often-stated quote from George Santayana, "Those who do not learn from history are doomed to repeat it." This is exactly the goal a good knowledge management program should embrace. The entire reason for your program's existence is to study and learn from the past and then share this knowledge.

The very same approach applies to knowledge management. The knowledge you gather and eventually disseminate is, at its core, a history. It is a review of a situation where one can learn from the past. It is a *lessons learned* from a mistake or near miss. It is a *case study* describing an in-depth *history* of a situation that can deliver the wisdom of the past.

History can be a *pack of lies* if not researched and recorded objectively. A good historian reviews the data very carefully and presents his/her findings with a detached impartiality. This isn't always an easy task because sometimes, even the best historians can have hidden, preconceived biases that even they are unaware of. Too often, a researcher goes into a project with a preconceived idea of what happened and then ends up writing the history behind the event to match their preconceived notions. This is exactly what Winston Churchill meant when he stated the winners write history, and they do so to justify their actions.

In order to manage knowledge properly, you need to become an historian. You need to be able to view the past objectively and with an open mind. The lessons learned that you catalog, and the case studies you write can be incredible tools to help make better decisions as well as prevent the same costly mistakes or, if poorly researched and written, can be nothing more than a *pack of lies* that provides the wrong message.

History is important; every intelligent discussion uses some form of history. Doctors rely on what treatment to prescribe by reviewing a patient's history. Juries review the history of a crime when deciding guilt or innocence, judges review court records before handing down a sentence, aerospace engineers look for past clues when preparing an accident report, and investment bankers thoroughly look at the past history of corporation and its management before investing in it.

If you think about it, almost every decision, even the simple minor ones you make each day, involve some sort of historical analysis. What route should you take to work today? Well, that depends on the road construction you encountered on yesterday's commute. What should we have for dinner tonight? That depends on what you had to eat over the past few days. History, understanding and learning from what happened in the past, is even a critical part our daily lives. This makes objective historical accounts all the more important.

Just as a good historian must use their critical judgment skills to objectively evaluate an historical event, so must a knowledge manager when searching for lessons learned. Sometimes, the facts may not be pleasant for an organization. For example, when the safety board appointed by Congress to review the loss of the Space Shuttle Columbia, NASA's management and culture came under a huge amount of public criticism. The report filed by the review board didn't mince words; it was an objective and nonpartisan history of a catastrophic accident. As we've seen, the objectivity and integrity displayed in the report's harsh assessment of NASA helped to fundamentally change the agency for the better.

History, if used properly, can be a tool that enables one to understand, judge, and make intellectually intelligent decisions. History gives better guidelines to make better judgments in the future. But it's a double-edged sword; history can be used improperly, and history that has opinion imposed becomes merely someone's propaganda or agenda.

As you set out to gather and produce knowledge, remember, objectivity and transparency are crucial. If the lessons you present and the case studies you compose contain such things as mistakes, small fabrications, or personal bias, you will lose your credibility with your customers, and once your integrity is questioned, it's almost impossible to regain. You must be unafraid of digging deep and exposing the mistakes made in the past.

Once you've begun gathering knowledge for your customers, the next step is disseminating that knowledge. At NASA, we learned from our experience with the ASAP who complimented us on our ability to gather critical knowledge but also criticized us for our inability to effectively share that knowledge with the workforce. Following are a variety of conduits we used to share the critical knowledge and history we learned from the past.

The Lessons Learned Database

The quickest and most customary way to gather and catalog knowledge is by developing an internal lessons learned database (LL). This can be accomplished in numerous ways, but the easiest is developing a simple-to-use template where employees can share information and describe their learning experience. It is important that all submissions to a lessons learned database go through a review or vetting process ensuring they are indeed pertinent and applicable as well as organized by topic. The database software you select needs to allow a search function so that the workforce can easily locate information they are looking for.

Lessons learned databases can be a significant tool used to gather and share knowledge. Lessons learned are generally a brief description of a specific bit of knowledge, for example, an entry warning that a certain supplier changed thread size in one of their components and production personnel need to make sure they don't use the wrong bolt and cross-thread the component, or another documented lesson learned might be a warning that unless a certain data entry keystroke method is used, significant omissions may occur during the entry process.

It's crucial to make your LL database easy to use and easy to locate. For any KM program, it will probably be the first place an employee looks when researching a problem. To make it successful, you'll need to encourage submissions to the database. All projects within your organization should be made aware of its existence and, because almost all lessons learned will come from these project team members, they should be encouraged to submit them. If employees are too busy or are uncomfortable writing, your KM office should provide assistance. At NASA, it was a requirement that all project teams document lessons learned. One good way for you to be aware of possible lessons learned is to track any engineering changes or process deviations that occur on a project because if they're changing something, it means, most likely, they found a problem and are trying to fix it. Another way is to keep in close contact with quality and assurance personnel; they should be able to provide a heads-up concerning changes being made on a project.

It's part of your job to make sure your workforce views lessons learned as an important tool that makes their jobs easier.

An example of a lessons learned database entry and what type of information may be needed is included in Appendix A.

Case Studies

The difference between a lessons learned and a case study is that a lesson learned is a brief description detailing a very specific problem and stating the precise fix to that problem. A case study is much more involved and complex. For example, the technical reason, or simple lesson learned, for the Space Shuttle Challenger failure was due to the faulty O-ring design of the solid rocket boosters. The O-rings were unable to seal the joints when exposed to freezing temperatures on the launch day. But the deeper, more complex reason for the Challenger catastrophe, and its viability as a case study, was due to the decision-making process as well as the organizational culture of NASA on that cold January morning. Fixing the O-ring joint on the solid rocket booster was easy; fixing the real cause for the tragedy was much more complex and difficult.

A case study is written like a story, a narrative, and describes a complex situation within the context in which an event, almost always an accident or failure, took place. The goal of a case study is to give the reader a much more comprehensive view of the complex systems as well as the complicated decision-making trees involved in a failure. A well-written case study engages the reader by placing him/her within the same settings and situations as the primary characters and not only makes them understand why the characters may have acted as they did but, more importantly, makes the reader question themselves and how they would react if standing in the character's shoes. A good case study makes the reader think.

A well-written case study can be an incredible learning tool when the reader is immersed within the entire context of an event and actually comes to understand the rationale, although proven faulty, used by the characters and makes the reader think: "Would I have done better?" When a reader begins to feel the emotional and human context within a failure or catastrophe, they tend to remember it much better than when simply being told the answer.

A carefully crafted case study can provide a significant enhancement to a training course, especially when incorporated with group discussions. We considered case studies to be so effective that we offered a technical writing workshop for engineers and project team members to help them develop and write case studies.

It's not always easy to write a case study, even if you have a very relevant topic in mind. Quite often, the person out in the field or on the shop floor who has an idea usually doesn't have the time or the training to write one. It's an excellent practice to help and encourage anyone in your workforce who needs technical writing help by offering assistance or training in case study design and writing. You may become impressed with the number of people in your organization who are interested in writing case studies and sharing their knowledge.

If you're looking for topics to write a case study around, your quality control or mission assurance office is usually a great place to start. These are the folks who are first notified when there's a problem, and they are also the ones who are responsible for performing the root cause analysis to uncover why and how the problem occurred.

Hints for writing a case study are as follows:

- As with every story, start with a strong opening, something that will engage the reader.
- You know what you want to get across—you know the solution to the problem you are describing, but you don't want to come out and state it as in a lesson learned entry. You want to give the reader all the data and information they need to come to the same conclusion on their own. This is a more active learning effort where the reader discovers the answer and thus feels more participative in the story and the solution.
- A good case study can provide a great opportunity for group discussion.
- Make it interesting. Know your audience, and when composing your case study, dig out facts that may be specific to their work and would intrigue them.
- Get your facts straight. One error or omission in your story could cause your reader to doubt the message you're trying to make. Doing research on the Web can be an incredible asset, but at the same time, there are lots of websites with inaccurate or outdated information.
- When researching your topic, be careful about newspaper descriptions. News articles can be unreliable because they are reporting an event as it is happening, and the reporter seldom has all the facts at such an early stage.
- In your case study, in the part of your story where you describe specific areas where problems occurred, such as poor decisions, point out the various options available before a flawed decision was made. It's critical to provide the context in which a decision had to be made so that the reader understands the complexity and depth of the problem being faced.

- Some case studies may only be applicable and relate to a certain, specific audience. But others can be universal in application. As we've seen, the Space Shuttle Challenger tragedy is more of a case study in a faulty decision-making process where employees felt compelled to yield their strong technical reservations to a management determined to launch. Every engineer can understand the technical cause, faulty O-ring joint design, but everyone, regardless of his or her occupation, can understand and identify with a decision process gone awry. The real learning message of the Challenger accident involves poor decisions and bad management practices rather than the O-ring failure.

- Bring in the human element and do your best to make the characters in your case study seem real. Make a reader feel like he/she is right there in the middle whether it be a launchpad or a boardroom.

- It's a bit of a balancing act, but be an objective writer. It's almost as if you are a lawyer explaining your case to a jury and trying to convince them of the truth. You want to make your case slowly and deliberately while laying out all the facts in a very concise and logical manner. As an author of a case study, your goal is to lead the reader to discover the truth on their own without forcing your opinions or views. Of course, you've thoroughly researched the subject matter and you know the answers, but you need to write your case study in a way that the reader comes to the same conclusion as yourself.

- Don't become discouraged if you think you have a good topic, and after a good deal of research, your thesis comes undone when you begin to fully understand the facts. Whatever you do, don't try to reshape the facts to meet your conclusion. Chalk it up to learning something new and look for another topic to write.

An example of a case study concerning the Concorde supersonic jet is included in Appendix B. At the time, in the 1960s, it was an incredible technological feat, yet there were signs right from the beginning of its development as well as throughout its operational lifespan that eventually, inevitably, led to its tragic crash in 2000. All it took was one avoidable and almost inconsequential event to ignite a chain reaction that left 109 people dead and ended the commercial supersonic flight.

Storytelling

Transforming a case study into an oral narrative can be a tremendous way to share critical knowledge. Storytelling can really make an impression that really sticks with a listener. Hearing a story, witnessing the storyteller, as well as being part of an audience affects the way we retain information and knowledge—it becomes more emotional because it's a shared experience.

Just like with developing a case study, consider yourself a lawyer making a case to a jury, only this time you're acting it out rather than writing it.

Not all case studies lend themselves to verbal stories. For example, highly technical issues seldom make for good oral presentations. The best stories are ones that involve people and can create emotions within your audience. These can be unforgettable learning moments. I'll never forget hearing a former shuttle program manager discuss his personal story involving the Columbia tragedy. He was part of the team that was reviewing videos of the foam impact strikes on the orbiter and trying to determine their locations and extent of the impacts. This manager told how he knew several of the astronauts on board Columbia and his daughter even attended grade school with a child of one of the astronauts. After Columbia disintegrated over the Texas skies, this manager, with a cracking voice and tears in his eyes, told how he was confronted by his daughter who asked, "Why did NASA kill my friend's daddy?" Emotional impacts like that, as well as the lesson you are trying to convey, stay with your audience.

Forums

Organizing learning events like forums can be an excellent way to share knowledge with the workforce. Forums can be large productions requiring an auditorium or much smaller, informal events such as brown bag listen-and-learn lunch events where project team members can share experiences.

Large forums can be beneficial opportunities for upper management to discuss critical issues before your company or organization. It's also an outstanding way for them to interact with the workforce as well as show their support for knowledge sharing.

One of the most significant forums we had delivered at NASA is the Space Shuttle Columbia Tour. This was a traveling road show that visited each NASA center throughout the country. We shipped a display case holding numerous artifacts recovered from the accident and held a two-hour forum inviting current NASA managers as well as mission controllers who were manning their stations that tragic morning, family members of the crew, and current astronauts, as well as other people who were involved in the Shuttle Program at the time of the accident. The idea was to make the forum a more personal experience by inviting those who were there when the tragedy took place, people who worked with and knew the crew. A forum like this can make engineers realize that the decisions made early in the design process may have a large impact later on when hardware is being manufactured and then operated. For NASA employees, this Space Shuttle Columbia forum also demonstrated how critical their work is when safety and human life are involved. The Columbia Tour Forum ensured that the lessons learned from this tragedy remained relevant in the minds of the NASA workforce, especially those who were too young or who were born after the accident.

Smaller forums can be interviews with project managers or entire project teams to discuss lessons from their projects. One very well-received topic and one that is particularly easy to organize is to invite leaders to discuss, *My Best Mistake*. This can create a dialog with employees who demonstrate that progress and success only happen after accepting mistakes are going to happen and understanding these mistakes offer a real opportunity for an organization to grow.

Video Interviews

Video knowledge capture can be an excellent vehicle to share knowledge. Lots of people are visual learners and prefer watching a video rather than reading a case study. Done right, video capture can provide quick access to numerous topics your customers need to be aware of.

At NASA, we produced two types of video knowledge sharing programs. The first were short informational video clips no more than 15 minutes long. There's little cost or prep time required as the person being interviewed can be in their office using their computer's camera or (pre-COVID) we'd tape it directly using a simple, inexpensive video camera. Short videos are perfect for discussing a general topic that you want to introduce to the viewer in hopes it leads them to look for more specific information, later. For example, short snippets describing the importance of good communication skills or the role of a systems engineer on a project team can appeal to a viewer's curiosity and lead them to utilize your KM and training resources for a more thorough explanation. Short clips like these, when searchable, can become a treasure trove of information that folks can quickly access.

The other type of video knowledge sharing event is somewhat longer and more involved than the 15-minute interviews. Long video discussions or forums should be done in a more relaxed setting such as on auditorium stage with large chairs and couches or a studio setting, if available. The idea is to interview several people on topics that require a much more in-depth platform. Usually, about an hour-long discussion hosted by a moderator and then Q&A from the live and online audience. This type of video production requires a lot more planning and staging and can be a bit stressful for many if done live, but it's an excellent way to convey knowledge.

At NASA, once a month, we developed an 1.5-hour-long live video webcast titled, Virtual Project Management Challenge. We would solicit our customers and stakeholders throughout the agency for relevant topics and issues, and then invite subject matter experts for a more detailed and comprehensive discussion. To make these productions more professional, we designed a format like a television talk show where a moderator, or host, would facilitate a relaxed discussion in a studio with comfortable chairs, good lighting, and a team of professional videographers, sound engineers, and network technicians.

Because it had such a professional look and shine, the Virtual Project Management Challenge gained a lot of popularity throughout NASA, and we were often asked by internal directorates and organizations to utilize this venue to get messages and information considered critical out to the workforce. For example, when the James Webb Space Telescope, a project that was approaching the $10 billion dollar mark, was having highly publicized technical issues the management of the Science Mission Directorate as well as the Human Exploration and Operations Directorate utilized our VPMC as a way to discuss lessons learned from large projects as well as openly discuss their strategy and plans to address difficult technical and programmatic issues.

Invitations to your stakeholders in upper management to participate in both short video clips and larger studio-like interviews is an excellent way to ensure they are getting their concerns out to the workforce, and it is a perfect way for your stakeholders to realize the value of your KM program.

Podcasts

Podcasts are another outstanding technique to transfer knowledge, particularly to the younger workforce within your organization who have grown up relying on this type of communication. This is a really inexpensive venue for knowledge sharing because the cost of the recording equipment and editing software is inconsequential in comparison to the value you can get from podcasting.

Some guests will feel much more comfortable being interviewed for a podcast rather than being videotaped, and there's a much quicker turnaround with a podcast than there is with video capture.

At NASA, there were literally hundreds of interesting people who could share a terrific story about their job, their career, their successes and failures in a 15-minute podcast. And a significant number of your customers will be drawn to your podcasts because it isn't a huge investment in their time. As a matter of fact, most of your listeners will download and listen during their downtime, for example, on their commute to work or while exercising or on a relaxing walk.

Podcasts can be placed on your website for downloading, and they can also be placed on a variety of external locations, without any costs, such as iTunes and Google where you can significantly broaden your audience.

Training Courses

One of the most important things we did at NASA to improve knowledge sharing was to integrate our KM office with our training office, the Academy of Program/Project and Engineering Leadership (APPEL).

APPEL was established after the Challenger accident when NASA management realized that advanced project management skills, as well as systems engineering capabilities, were necessary to better manage the growing number of complex projects within the agency. APPEL started out with a few introductory courses, but as NASA's portfolio of space and aeronautic projects grew, APPEL invested in a more robust training program that included a curriculum of over 50 courses, as well as consulting services to enhance project performance. Over time, APPEL has been considered one of the premier training organizations in the federal government and has collected numerous awards, including, *Best Academy in the World* by Human Systems International, an organization that benchmarks project management training throughout the world.

By combining knowledge management with APPEL, we instantly gained credibility and exposure for our fledgling knowledge management program. Engineers, by their very nature, like to learn new things and, because project management and systems engineering are not covered thoroughly in an undergraduate engineering program, almost every NASA engineer has been exposed to APPEL training sometime in their careers.

What better conduit to share lessons learned and critical corporate knowledge than training courses? After all, isn't training at its very essence knowledge sharing?

By integrating KM with APPEL, we also gained flexibility, particularly with our budget, because now we were partners in sharing knowledge, and training is just one part of that overall goal to develop a stronger agency by incorporating a complete knowledge management strategy.

At NASA, the workforce was composed primarily of engineers, so it might be assumed that APPEL offered a lot of courses involving complex math and aerospace engineering, but that is not at all the case. NASA hires very smart people, and its engineers acquired their math and engineering skills very effectively while earning their undergraduate degrees.

What a lot of the workforce needed, particularly new hires, was training that they did not get while earning their bachelors. APPEL created what we called the *Fifth Year Program*, which, after a lot of discussions with university professors and new graduates, was a collection of topics and courses that they should have been exposed to had their undergraduate experience been extended an extra year. This was done under the premise that four years is not enough time to fully develop a mature engineer who was ready to immediately step into the workforce at NASA. In other words, there were other professional qualities they needed such as effective communication skills, leadership and team membership skills, and an understanding of NASA through its history and legacy.

In order to teach a thorough understanding of NASA, the Fifth Year Program included a new set of courses to help our newly hired graduates learn the critical lessons from NASA's past. In the development of this new curriculum, we quickly realized that nearly all the lessons learned and case studies involving failure, very few are caused by computational errors. Most are caused by judgmental and decision-making mistakes. Most engineering failures are the result of human error.

These new courses offered the perfect opportunity to bring knowledge management into training, and it highlighted the benefits of integrating KM with education. Though, these courses were designed in a heuristic fashion to make the NASA workforce aware of a more comprehensive, inclusive approach when making decisions where numerical data might not suffice. All these courses included numerous real case studies, which helped reinforce the importance of developing and using critical thinking skills.

This new curriculum was titled, "Lesson Learned for Mission Success" and some of the offerings were as follows.

Cognitive Bias in the Engineering Decision-Making Process

- We explored the decision-making process and the effects of such issues as cognitive bias, a situation that an individual may not even be aware of, but they've already made up their mind in advance. How to avoid problems like *group think*, mental shortcuts, and biases of optimism that can compromise our ability to make sound judgments, especially in critical situations. (As I am writing this, we are engaged in the worldwide COVID-19 pandemic, and every time I venture out to the grocery store and witness the empty shelves that once held paper products, I am reminded of *group think* where irrational fear causes panic buying.)

Quiet Project Management

- A large part of many technical workforces tend to have varying degrees of introverted personalities. In order to build strong teams and ensure effective communication among all project team members, we designed a course to help our employees to better understand how to work and communicate effectively while working together. We also placed a large emphasis demonstrating the importance of speaking up and expressing your opinion on any issue, especially those involving quality and safety.

Critical Thinking and Problem-Solving

- Utilizing case studies, participants to this course were given real problems faced by a variety of past project managers and team members and must decide the best way to move forward to achieve mission success. Numerous group exercises were conducted in techniques such as analytics, strategy, innovation, avoiding decision-making biases, and creative thinking skills.

Pay It Forward: Capturing, Sharing, and Learning NASA Lessons

- This was a one-day seminar to encourage employees to utilize and get the most out of the NASA lessons learned database. What constitutes an effective lesson learned, where to find the information you need by conducting a relevant search, and how to compose an entry for the database.

Complex Decision Making in Project Management

- Using numerous NASA case studies, attendees studied in detail how real-world decisions within large high-profile programs and projects costing millions of dollars were effected by such things as erroneous data, indecision, overconfidence, political influences, and the lack of a rigorous decision-making process. We also focused on encouraging managers to be open toward the diversity of thought and experiences presented within a project team. This wide variety of expertise, experience, and opinion should be valued and utilized during the decision process.

Case Study Workshop

- During this one-day workshop, employees came prepared with a topic they thought suitable for a case study and are then tutored by a professional technical writer how to transform it into an engaging, relevant story. Once completed, it could be considered for our catalog of case studies and uploaded to our website.

The Lessons Learned for Mission Success curriculum was an attempt to develop critical thinking skills, as well as challenge our technical workforce to broaden their outlook. Too often, many become too comfortable and content viewing the world through the eyes of an engineer. Away from the test stands, flight hardware, and computer terminals, there exists a very different world that, at times, can appear much more complex and puzzling but where an engineer must also prevail to make correct and responsible decisions.

Putting It All Together: an Integrated Website

Once you've gathered all the information that you deem critical for your organization's success, how do you make it easily accessible? You need a one-stop-shop website, a centralized location where everyone in your organization knows they can go to find the knowledge they need as quickly as possible.

Your customers are busy people, so it is imperative that your website design is made as simple and easy to navigate as possible. Everything available should be easily located on your homepage. Categorize everything you offer to your customers in a logical, consistent order. For example, one button for the course catalog, another button for the lessons learned database, another for podcasts, another for case studies, and so on. Design it so one quick look and a click and they have what they're looking for.

You want your workforce to get the information they need with a minimal number of clicks. There are few things as frustrating as a poorly designed website that causes the user to continually click around to find what they're looking for. Use simple, concise, direct wording that easily explains each function of the website. How many times on the Web have you come across phrases or wording that is so technical in nature that you're left wondering what it even means?

And finally, do everything you can to fight off the website developers innate inclination for fancy bells and whistles. Website innovation for the sake of innovation makes for confusion and frustration. Your customers come to your website for answers, not IT shock and awe.

Newsletter: Spreading the Word

Developing an e-mail distribution list and a short, concise monthly newsletter describing the efforts made by your KM office can be an excellent way to share knowledge and keep the workforce and management—your customers and stakeholders—aware of your progress. A distribution list can easily be created within your organization, and you can also offer subscriptions to your newsletter directly on your website. At NASA, we sent out a monthly update on new case studies, lessons learned, courses, and video capture with links directly back to our website. The distribution list has grown to over 60,000 subscribers worldwide.

Social Media

The wide variety of social media sites makes it much easier to market your KM efforts and it's totally free. Without a doubt, LinkedIn can be an exceptional venue to share case studies and other knowledge products your team has developed. LinkedIn can be a valuable tool to develop professional contacts and insights, as well as an international platform to draw attention to your KM organization's success.

Opening a Twitter account allows you to give live streaming reports during knowledge events, as well as receive questions from a broad, world-wide audience. The exposure on such platforms as Facebook can also help generate a growing KM program. Information now travels at the speed of light, and your customers all carry cellphones that can become knowledge tools when you manage your KM utilizing the many opportunities available within social media.

Collaboration

Collaborating is a two-way street where you can help another organization and, at the same time, they can help yours. There's a lot of organizations, both internal and external, out there trying to get a handle on managing knowledge. At NASA, we took collaboration seriously and always looked for opportunities because it's helpful in two ways; you can always learn from others and gain new ideas or processes and you can also benchmark your progress against theirs.

Internal collaboration can reap a wide number of benefits. By working and assisting other departments within your organization, your KM program can gain support where you need it most, with your organization's stakeholders. For example, at NASA, an employee of the Office of Equal Opportunity and Diversity attended our *Cognitive Bias in Engineering Decision-Making* course and asked us to help them develop a similar course but based more upon cognitive biases related to diversity. Another example involved NASA History Office, which was trying to gain attendance at their monthly *Brown Bag Talks*. By simply posting a notice on our website (which was getting over 24,000 hits each month), we were able to almost triple the number of attendees to their lunchtime talks. By supporting these efforts, as well as many others, we gained influential support within NASA management.

The NASA KM and training program also developed a strong external stature, not only because we earned several awards, but also because we were always willing to benchmark our program with other organizations, both governmental and corporate, throughout the world. Domestically, I have met with KM executives from DoD, the Federal Bureau of Investigation, Department of Energy, the National Science Foundation, and many others, as well as various international space agencies, institutes, and companies. After each one of these external benchmarks, we would see a significant spike in hits on our website. Collaborating is a great way to learn and share with others as well as build your program's reputation.

Investigate other companies and agencies that are involved in knowledge management and set up meetings and benchmarking sessions where you can share your successes, opportunities and difficulties and learn from theirs. Don't limit your KM connections to organizations that are working in a similar industry or market as your own. You'd be surprised how much insight you can gain from benchmarking with an organization outside of your specific field or product line. Outside organizations in other markets may look at issues in a different light and may take an approach you never considered because you've been entrenched within your organization's way of doing things for such a long time. For example, we were conducting a succession planning study and gained some great insights from the airline industry and how they prepare for the loss of highly trained and skilled pilots. Some of their processes for growing and developing internal talent were directly applicable to NASA's highly trained and skilled engineering workforce. Note: you can usually tell your KM office is garnering respect if you get outside requests to benchmark.

Metrics

A significant and effective way of measuring your KM program's success is to develop a set of useful metrics. The benefit of having a one-stop-shop website is that you don't have to look far to gather your metrics; most of everything you need will be easily retrieved from monitoring the number of hits, the number of views to the various pages on your site, number of downloads of case studies, video interviews, podcasts, and so on. One important metric we kept a close eye on each month was the number of new submissions to our lessons learned database along with the number searches to the database and topics garnering the most searches.

Each month, I would request a metrics report from our leads showing such data as number of courses held and number attendees, number of website hits, as well as the most popular page viewed, along with the lessons learned database info. This report was compiled with charts and graphs into a PowerPoint presentation, which I would forward to my manager keeping him informed of our progress.

Gathering and sharing knowledge are critical components of a healthy, vibrant organization. You don't have to look far within your organization for knowledge. Every employee on your payroll has some degree of critical knowledge that helps your organization operate efficiently. It might be the guy on the assembly line who, after years of performing countless repetitive actions, has figured out an easier and more efficient way to insert pistons into an engine block, a procedure the industrial engineers never thought of. It may be the data entry person who stumbled upon a hidden feature in the operating system that allows them to add five times as many entries, or it could be the special technique a salesman has discovered to convince potential customers that they need your product.

The nice thing is that all this information or knowledge is right there in front of you, and it's free for the taking. The bad part is, there's a real sense of urgency to gather and share this knowledge because once this employee moves on to another role within your company or another position at another company, this knowledge may be gone forever. That's why, knowledge sharing, and the various venues of disseminating this critical, corporate knowledge is so important to your organization's success.

In this chapter, you learned the following:

> - To manage knowledge, you must act as a historian. You not only need to filter information to refine knowledge, but before you begin the important step of sharing that knowledge, you need to make certain it is objectively recorded and presented clearly and concisely. The knowledge you present is going to be used by your audience/ customers to make critical decisions. You need to ensure what you present is truthful and useful.

- A lessons learned database can be a valuable tool for your workforce to locate critical data; therefore, you must make certain the database contains pertinent lessons learned, and they are easily searchable.
- Lessons learned are different from case studies. A lesson learned generally describes a simple fix to a specific problem, whereas a case study describes a longer and more complex situation where usually, a series of difficulties developed into a much more serious problem. A well-written case study that concisely describes a problem and also addresses the personal and human emotions that were encountered to solve the problem can make a personal impression and positively impact the reader throughout their career.
- There are numerous ways to share knowledge, forums, storytelling, podcast interviews, social media, and so on, but the most important and effective venue is incorporating KM within training courses.
- Metrics not only show you what your customers think of your program but they also offer a great opportunity to share your success with your stakeholders in upper management.

Questions to consider are as follows:

- Does your organization collect and catalog lesson learned? Is it utilized by your workforce? If not, is it because it is cumbersome to locate information or contains lessons that are really superfluous to the workforce?
- Does your organization offer training courses? Is there an opportunity for you to incorporate critical knowledge within this coursework?
- Case studies are used everywhere to get an important message across to an audience. Are there topics within your organization that could be developed into case studies? Are their qualified people on your staff to research and write them?

CHAPTER 7

Problems You Will Encounter

The First Rule of Project Management

Remember this as your first rule toward developing a successful program, and not just a KM program but any program—without upper management support, you will inevitably fail. Period. You may have developed a stellar foundation for KM and be sitting on a goldmine of helpful lessons learned and fascinating case studies, but without stakeholder and champion support, your hard work and enthusiasm will be doomed, and to make things even worse, once your KM program fails, it will be seen in the same light as other failed programs in the project management dustbin.

This is why, it's absolutely critical to keep your stakeholders and champions in the loop concerning your activities and successes. If you're gathering monthly metrics, share them and always make your knowledge sharing venues open and available for upper management to participate as speakers, presenters, or hosts. Make your KM program feel like theirs.

At NASA, as mentioned earlier, the chief knowledge officer was an advisor and reported directly to the agency's chief engineer, and both training and knowledge management were located in the office of the chief engineer. This is an excellent arrangement that keeps the chief engineer and other technical managers informed of KM activities and opens opportunities for their participation. Being located in the office of the chief engineer also sent a message to the workforce: NASA management supports and considers training and knowledge management as critical functions.

You Can Lead a Horse to Water but Can't Make It Drink...

Unfortunately, it can also work both ways. You may have strong stakeholder support, great internal, corporate knowledge, and good internal platforms ready to share but find yourself with little customer support—you just can't seem to get the people who need the information most to utilize it. This is where it really gets frustrating. People may be too busy to access your treasure trove of knowledge or add to it by submitting lessons learned and pointing out case study topics. The only answer is to keep pushing the value KM brings and prove your value by promoting success stories where your program helped a project team. Demonstrating upper management's support by their participation in KM events is also a sure-fire way to get your customer's attention and participation.

Feedback: Criticism From Customers

You will soon notice that almost everyone has an opinion on knowledge management and especially, training. "The customer is always right!" is a smart way to manage a retail store, restaurant, and your knowledge management office, but, with some reservations. The trick is having an objective outlook to your own work. Always be open to suggestions, but at the same time, keep in mind that just because someone has an opinion, it doesn't mean their opinion is necessarily right. Of course, listen to your customers, particularly when they have criticisms concerning content, but you'll find a lot of superfluous comments that you really have no control over, such as the "room was too cold," "there wasn't enough coffee," and "the chairs were uncomfortable." Don't let this type of criticism bother you or disrupt your progress, instead concentrate on the more consequential feedback you receive.

As described earlier, customer service is a critical component of your KM office. Part of customer service includes gathering feedback from your customers and your stakeholders. Before reviewing feedback, it's important to take a step back and be as objective as possible. This isn't always easy after putting so much of your time and efforts into developing your program, but constructive criticism can make your program even better.

At NASA, we placed a great deal of emphasis on customer satisfaction, and after each knowledge sharing event or class, conducted a very thorough evaluation followed by an event *lessons learned* meeting. We sorted through the complaints that are beyond our control ("The cafeteria was too far away and I couldn't get back to the class in time"), and instead, studied the more thoughtful responses and always looked for ways to improve. There have been numerous times we've incorporated a customer's suggestion into our programs. For example, we send out e-mail notices for upcoming knowledge sharing events a week beforehand. One suggestion we got was to add a button on our e-mail that, when clicked, would place the event into the recipient's electronic calendar so they wouldn't forget. It took our web design folks a minimal amount of time to incorporate this helpful suggestion into future e-mail reminders.

Feedback: Criticism From Stakeholders

This is a bit more difficult when the people holding the purse strings or wielding the power in your organization have negative feedback. It's always critical to keep your management informed on a project's progress, but with KM, that becomes a bit more difficult because, unlike the other project within your organization that are manufacturing widgets and can easily show production numbers and other quantitative data, you have a much more difficult time demonstrating your success through production data or the return on investment value that management uses to judge most programs. Obviously, you are at a disadvantage, but there are some things you can do: use your customer feedback to justify your program. Your stakeholders need to see how the money spent on your (their) KM program may not be immediately affecting the organization's bottom line, but in the long run is strengthening their organization. Here's some areas to consider:

- Metrics, metrics, metrics. Gather customer feedback from you KM activities. Utilize the registration process to collect attendee info such as their job function, the project they are assigned to, and their job classification. Use metrics to find out who is utilizing your program and verify they are the same folks you identified as your customers.

- Develop some pre- and postsurvey questions of attendees that demonstrate how much more they learned about a topic because they attended your event.
- Listen closely to your stakeholders for suggested topics they want included in your KM efforts and always try to get them to attend, or better yet, present during learning events.
- As mentioned previously, collaborate internally. Talk with other departments and always offer to help. The resulting positive feedback and the influential allies you and your organization build can pay dividends when upper managers meet behind closed doors. Collaboration helps solidify your program's importance within the organization.

The Great Debate: eLearning Versus In-Person Knowledge Sharing

Be prepared for that one manager who tries to push the idea that all training and knowledge sharing events can be *modernized* or *streamlined* by making all learning virtual and online. It wasn't so long ago that electronic learning was predicted to be such a revolutionary development in education that it would soon supplant the traditional classroom experience in our colleges and universities, but this, of course, never happened. Electronic learning has its place, but in most cases, it cannot replace the face-to-face instructional experience a course or forum taught by a subject matter expert or the inherent personal value of group networking and discussion.

Sometimes, it's claimed that the new generation of employees prefers *learning on the go* and desktop training rather than instructor-led learning. There is some value to that statement, certainly some forms of training and knowledge sharing can very effectively be done online, but you have to be sensible when selecting what is appropriate for eLearning. Quick hits like podcasting or short video interviews can be very effective, but complex topics that require a large degree of expertise are better off remaining in a traditional in-person format.

Yes, instructor-led learning and knowledge events may come with a large initial price tag, but there are also a lot of hidden costs involved with eLearning. For example, to do a respectable job videotaping an event, you'll usually need three cameras, a lighting, and audio technician, and of course, someone with an understanding of the material being presented in order to edit all the video into a coherent program. In a lot of cases, once editing is completed, the videotape has to have the audio portion transcribed for the hearing impaired before it can be shown. And, of course, should the subject matter ever require updating, you will need to either re-edit or completely redo your eLearning event.

You can also use a hybrid approach to training and sharing knowledge by developing a webcast that combines a subject matter expert presenting live to a broad audience through a network connection, which also allows for audience interaction via a Q&A session at the end. But it comes with some risk; you'll need rock-solid network equipment with a large bandwidth and the expertise to manage it. Too often, connections go out, or audio becomes garbled, and it can become an extremely distracting experience for your Internet audience. If network problems happen too often, it can become so frustrating that your customers may not even bother accessing your online learning events in the future.

Over the years, I've had a steady stream of managers recommend all training and knowledge sharing events should be eLearning, and over those same years, I have never had an attendee to a course or forum state they would have preferred it to attend it or view it remotely. There's something about face-to-face interaction and the rapport that develops during these interactions that makes the training or sharing knowledge experience much more effective.

Be Aware of Personal Sensitivity

You're going to run into problems in your quest to gather and share knowledge. Lots of people are reluctant to discuss past mistakes and lessons learned, especially if they cost the organization a large amount of money or caused personal or corporate embarrassment. There is no easy solution other than continually emphasizing that no one is casting blame but rather trying to demonstrate the importance of learning from the past.

Most people resent being pointed out for doing something wrong, let alone having their mistake(s) revealed and made an example in front of their peers and co-workers. Just try pointing out a mistake your spouse or significant other may have made and then follow that up by publicly documenting a lesson learned from their error and see what kind of reaction you get. Most people are very sensitive about the past errors they have committed.

You can't allow sharing lessons about failures to become blame game because no one will participate. As a KM professional, it is critical to develop a culture within your organization that is careful and sensitive about judging those individuals who unfortunately had to learn lessons the hard way. No one wants to make a mistake, but if we can learn from it, we can grow and move forward more confidently. As Dean Martin once reminded us with his humor: "Good judgment comes from experience. And experience? Well, that comes from poor judgment." Learn from other's mistakes.

Conspiracy Theories

Be careful, people love a good conspiracy theory, and in this day and age, they are so prevalent that they've almost become a part of our everyday life to such an extent that we'll spend too much time actually analyzing some, even though we know they are ridiculous.

Conspiracy theories are not based on facts, they rely on the absence of facts to derive a semblance of reasonableness. For example, some conspiracy theorists have speculated that President Reagan demanded that the Space Shuttle Challenger be launched despite the contrary advice NASA managers made on that fateful, freezing cold morning of January 28, 1986. The theory goes that the president overruled flight managers because he was going to present his state of the union address that evening and wanted to highlight his administration's achievement of launching the first teacher in space. Well, at a first glance, it sounds reasonable (especially if you didn't care for President Reagan), but the theory is accompanied by no facts, it's simply a *possibility*, which is never permissible when documenting lessons learned. The really dangerous component of conspiracy theories is that by just mentioning it, you instantly supply some sort of credibility to it in some peoples' mind. (Just to make sure I don't do that with the preceding example, the Rogers Commission, which investigated the Challenger disaster, ruled out such an occurrence because there was exactly no evidence to support it.)

Cognitive Biases

There's a whole lot of different biases involved in decision making, and for our purposes, we won't cover them all here, but we do need to point out a couple that need to be considered when researching and gathering knowledge for sharing.

- Confirmation bias: This is when someone enters a discussion or investigation with their mind already made up. They have a purely subjective outlook, and rather than looking for the truth are, instead, looking for evidence that verifies or backs up their opinion. Be careful; sometimes, people only see what they want to see.
- Hindsight bias occurs when someone looks back at the myriad of complex events that led to a failure and believes these events were clearly foreseeable and could have been easily avoided. This hubris is the result, not of some keen ability to understand complex systems, but due simply to hindsight, which we all know is 20/20. Hindsight bias is prevalent almost everywhere and in almost every situation where cause and effect are being investigated. How many times have you watched a coach call a trick play that fails miserably, and you find yourself screaming about such a stupid call? You've judged the coach's call only because you already have seen the outcome. But if the trick play works, all of a sudden, you view your team's coach as a genius.

The Apollo I fire that caused three astronauts to lose their lives was discovered to be the result of using 100 percent oxygen in the capsule's atmosphere. After the tragedy, many people thought it was insane to design the interior that would present such an incredible risk for fire. What they don't realize is that a capsule design with typical Earth atmosphere of 78 percent nitrogen and 21 percent oxygen would require another separate, heavy tank for the nitrogen in an already crowded capsule design. Too bad hindsight will always beat foresight. Some things just aren't as simple as they first appear.

- The good old days bias. Nostalgia… How many times has someone tapped the thick steel hood of an old classic car and say, "They sure don't build 'em like they used to!" No, they sure don't, thank God. Those old cars were completely unreliable and incredibly inefficient, unsafe, and uncomfortable compared to today's cars. We tend to forget that tires wore out after only 5,000 miles, and tuning a carburetor was a constant chore that, despite constant tweaking, never seemed to get the engine to run smoothly. In the *good old days*, if you were in a serious accident, you seldom had a chance of surviving, while today's cars are designed for keeping passengers as safe as possible. Remembering the past with rose-colored glasses almost always results in an inaccurate view comparing the past to the present.

When gathering knowledge and assessing current situations and then comparing them to the past, keep in mind the context of the past. Yes, the sheet metal was much thicker on the hood of that car, but the designers of that 1960 Ford weren't a bit concerned about gas mileage, efficiency, or longevity.

Learning Your Lesson Too Well

Sometimes, particularly after a catastrophic event, you learn your lesson too well and become almost paralyzed. This can happen when a person, or an entire organization, becomes panic-stricken at the fear of creating another failure. As a result, they develop an overly cautious approach, which in turn endangers success and inevitably stifles innovation and creativity. No one wants to make a mistake, but progress isn't accomplished without some level of risk. As the famed NASA flight controller Gene Krantz once wrote, "There is no achievement without risk."

It's the role of the knowledge management team to help develop an internal culture that ensures an organization will grow stronger and more effective by learning from the past. Mistakes and failures are going to happen. Name one person or organization that has never had a failure. The ones that have addressed their failure openly and objectively and put in place processes to prevent it from happening again are the ones that not only survive but excel.

Scope Creep: Putting Lean KM at Risk

If a knowledge management program is left undisciplined and unfocused, its scope can slowly grow, or creep, to such levels that it can become unmanageable, resulting in a whole lot of something for no one. You must continually remind yourself who your customers are and what they need. We live in a world inundated with information, and if you leave the door open too wide and broaden your scope beyond what your customers need, you're going get information overload.

Scope creep can often be found with the introduction of new IT tools such as new hi-tech search engines or new software databases. These tools are usually in the development stage, and their sponsors may be looking at you as a test bed or even as a funding source. Mind you, these tools can all show promise, but if you want to stay lean, you need to avoid them until they've matured.

As mentioned previously, one of the best defenses against scope creep is a very concise and unambiguous project plan that clearly defines your audience as well as your KM project's goals and requirements.

Hijacking the Truth

It may feel good and be reassuring to think, in the end that, "the truth shall prevail," but unfortunately, it's also a bit naive. Sometimes, an individual or even an entire organization may find it convenient or profitable to twist the truth to meet their agenda. There are countless examples of individuals and organizations twisting the truth, or even completely falsifying it in order to promote their agenda. Ever hear of Enron? How about Dieselgate? Unfortunately, it happens more often that we'd like to know.

And sometimes, it is the falsehoods that prevail, and when they do, they can cause long-lasting consequences. Almost every school child has been taught that Christopher Columbus discovered that the earth was round when he sailed for the New World. But, in reality, back in the 15th century, most learned people had already accepted the earth was round, and ancient Greeks and Egyptians had mathematically proven it centuries beforehand. If you look at paintings of kings and queens during Columbus' time and even before, you'll notice royal coats of arms featuring a round globe or royal scepters with a globe carved atop representing their imperial sovereignty.

Well, then why has the Christopher Columbus story lingered on? It all stems from a book written over 200 years ago, *A History of the Life and Voyages of Christopher Columbus,* by Washington Irving. In his book, Irving portrayed the people of Columbus' time as all believing the world was flat, and if a ship sailed too far west, its terrified sailors would fall off the side into the abyss.

Why would Irving write a history that was so patently false? Well, the author had an agenda. Irving was passionately anti-Catholic and used his story as a platform to demean the Church as virulently backward in its attempts to stop Irving's hero Columbus. Washington Irving sought to demonstrate that Columbus was a new type of man, a man of science who had to struggle against the reactionary Church.

Despite a huge amount of contrary historical fact, Washington Irving's story that Christopher Columbus discovered the world was round is still ingrained in most people.

Spontaneous Knowledge Sharing

Depending how large your organization may be, you're likely to see pockets of knowledge gathering and sharing occurring sometimes without your awareness such as *Lunch and Learn* gatherings or project teams hosting their own lessons learned event. Your initial reaction may be to try to control these spontaneous events or even stop them, but I think a more reasonable approach is to understand the good intentions of these people and offer to help them. You can't control everything, especially within a large organization. People, by nature, are going to want to share what they've learned and might not always go through the proper channels to do so. Stopping them because they didn't follow the process will send the wrong message, and it will actually appear you are preventing knowledge sharing—not something you want your stakeholders to get wind of! Perhaps, the better attitude is to help them and realize that your program is responsible for creating a culture where people feel free to share what they've learned.

Situations Out of Your Control

I once had a very open but disconcerting conversation with the lead training officer for a major automobile manufacturer. In the course of our discussion, I mentioned I owned one of their models, and I recently had to pay almost $2,000 to have the engine head gaskets replaced. As I researched this particular problem, I discovered it was a known issue with this car model, and there were rants about it (and the repair costs) all over the Internet. I remarked, "You guys have been building cars for almost a hundred years, how could it be possible that you could design and manufacture a faulty head gasket?" There was a bit of a pause on the line, and then he replied, "Actually, in a lot of situations the lawyers get involved. Over the years we've had devastating lawsuits and lawyers look at engineering documentation as potential incriminating evidence, so they ask us to destroy it. A lot of this documentation includes critical test results that, in the hands of a clever personal injury lawyer, can appear damning to the company." So, what happened is they became selective on what knowledge to retain. What further complicates the situation is the snowball effect that can happen when a person who has been designing, let's say head gaskets, retires and now there is the authentic risk that the organization has set themselves up for failure because the critical documentation and knowledge has been destroyed.

This is a compelling sort of Catch-22 problem. In order not to get sued, destroy potential damaging engineering documentation and then, without having proper engineering documentation, continue designing and manufacturing defective products, which then causes a loss of customers, company credibility, profit, and of course, numerous lawsuits.

Developing Hubris

Herbert Butterfield, the former distinguished historian at Cambridge University, taught that historical events and people must be viewed within the context of their time, and it was wrong to judge from the advantage of hindsight and looking back from the future. Butterfield wrote, "A twentieth century school-boy could make some of the founders of modern science look foolish… It is necessary that we should always measure such thinkers against the state of things which preceded them—not against the twentieth century."

We should extend Professor Butterfield's attitude of humility toward the people and the context of the events they faced in the past to our own study of learning lessons from the mistakes made in the past. Everything becomes quite obvious when you have the advantage of retrospection, but it's necessary, and helpful to understanding exactly what happened, when you put yourself in the shoes of the person involved in a mistaken decision or mishap from the past.

There are times when people involved in KM gain a bit of hubris because they possess the distinct advantage of retrospection. They research a case study and make judgments on past people and decisions from the comfort of their warm offices and cushioned chairs and not in the context of the times where, perhaps, the decision makers didn't have all the information they needed or the data they were given was erroneous. Our job is to share the lessons the folks from the past had to learn the hard way, not to appear gloating from our distinct advantage of hindsight.

It's real easy to look back at, for example, the Space Shuttle Challenger disaster and say to oneself, "What were they thinking?" But it's a lot harder to place yourself within the shoes of the people who were involved in the fateful decision to launch. You don't want to make excuses for poor decisions, but at the same time, you want to be as objective as possible and describe and understand the context under which these people had to make the decisions they did. You're not going to teach the real lesson you want your audience to learn unless you place them within the situational context of the time.

It becomes even more problematic when your KM organization is viewed as possessing a bit of hubris when presenting a case study or facilitating a discussion. Those working on the front lines, those having to make critical decisions and evaluate risk will justifiably lose patience and respect when they see themselves being second-guessed or judged by others who never had to deal with the type of pressure they're under.

In this chapter, you learned the following:

- The hard lesson of project management always remains this: without upper management's support, you will have a very difficult, if not impossible task ahead of you. You need to gain that support and nurture it through your continued success.
- Feedback is important, but it needs to be refined a bit, just like you refine information into real knowledge. Everyone has an opinion on training and knowledge management, but if you stick with your cardinal tenet—supporting your defined audience—you will have an easier time deciphering and determining useful feedback.
- No one likes having their mistakes pointed out in a public forum. Be cognizant of this when sharing the lessons learned of a failed or troubled project and always be on guard against developing a sense of superiority or hubris when explain past failures.
- Cognitive bias is everywhere, and it's also very difficult to detect. As stated before, you are an historian and your job is to present the facts objectively. You always want to convey the right message.
- One effect of a successful program is growth. Your lean KM program can grow and still remain lean if you remember to focus only on your customers and avoid scope creep.

Questions to consider are as follows:

- As stated previously, customer support and listening to your customers is critical to success. Can you differentiate between real constructive criticism and criticism that is mostly just a form of background noise?
- Within your organization's culture, is it possible to explain a lesson learned or develop a case study describing a failure without it morphing into a tribunal or inquiry?
- Do you have the project management discipline to avoid scope creep and stick to your objective, that is, focusing on your customers?

CHAPTER 8

Lean Knowledge Management: Areas for Growth

As your knowledge management office becomes successful, you may begin to see other areas for growth within your organization that can be improved with KM while still staying within the boundaries of your project plan. You can grow and still remain lean by remembering to concentrate solely on your customers and by continually supporting your stakeholders.

Embedded CKO

On large projects or programs that are crucial to your organization's success, it can be a real asset to permanently embed a chief knowledge officer. This CKO's full time role could provide three critical functions: first, to be the project's historian, to document every phase of the project and record the success and difficulties encountered so that these lessons can be accurately shared in the future. Second, an embedded CKO could be a resource for the project team when problems are encountered by researching past strategies and remedies to the issues. And, finally, as we saw earlier in the discussion of a KM chain of command, the embedded CKO could be a direct link, especially in a large program with matrixed management structure (as most large programs are), to his/her leadership by helping them understand the issues being encountered as well as the plans being put in place to deal with them.

Assisting Your Organization's Leadership

Those at the very top in your organization's chain of command, those who make the critical decisions impacting everyone's future may benefit the most from KM's lessons from the past.

For example, how does a company deal with the publicity and fallout from a major disaster or scandal? A strong KM program can be used to discover such crucial answers by researching how other organizations in the past dealt with such crises. There's plenty to study, such as, the Deepwater Horizon oil spill in the Gulf of Mexico, the Exxon Valdez oil tanker spill off Prince William Sound, Alaska, Union Carbide's response to the Bhopal industrial disaster, Three Mile Island, or of course, the Challenger and Columbia tragedies. A simple Google search and *industrial accidents* pulls up hundreds of possibilities, and each one of them may have some lessons your leadership can learn from.

Being prepared to give your leadership the lessons from the past can enable them to see what strategy went right and what went wrong and enable them to avoid the accidents of the past and make the right decisions for your organization. One option is to develop a special course or workshop for upper management that utilizes appropriate case studies dealing with strategic decision making and leadership and gives them an insight into successfully handling some of the major issues they may encounter.

Succession Planning as a Function of KM

Look at your top leadership, is your organization prepared for their departure? What's more critical for an organization's future than that? There's several ways KM can help upper management prepare for the inevitable change that will take place at every level of decision-making roles within their organization. Preparing new people to fill these roles, people who need to understand the organization's culture, strategies, and marketplace is crucial for smooth transitions.

- Mentoring: Bring young people who possess leadership potential into the offices of upper management to attend high-level meetings and work directly with the critical managers who lead your organization. Incorporate temporary details where a high potential employee can accompany a high-performing manager for several weeks or even months to witness how decisions are made and how the organization operates. Such an experience obviously helps a younger employee feel more comfortable with upper management and enables them an opportunity to learn how the organization operates, but it also works both ways because the manager gets to know and understand how a new generation of leaders thinks and can see, first-hand, what motivates and energizes them. Upper management might also be able to pick up some helpful hints and tips as far as social media and reaching out and communicating with a new generation of workers.

- Leadership programs: Leadership training can be criticized because of its cost, but look at it this way: it is an investment. There's a difference between cost and investment. We invest money to make more money, and when we invest in leadership training, it shouldn't be viewed as a *cost*, it should be viewed as an investment in the future that will provide organizational success that leads to making more money.

Subject Matter Database

A good KM program knows where to find the subject matter experts within its organization. Compiling a searchable list of names and contact information can provide easy and quick access to someone who has the expertise to solve problems. Make this database prominent on your KM website so that if any employee needs help or advice, they know right where to go.

Onboarding New Hires

As stated previously, knowledge management's first and most critical act is to determine who their audience is and to develop the program to meet their needs. KM can be the best provider for relaying a snapshot of how an organization is structured and what it needs to operate effectively, but KM can teach new hires about the organization's history, so they can learn from the past, even though they're new employees. A good KM onboarding can be developed to ensure the values, traditions, and legacy of your organization will be passed onto your newer KM customers.

One early career effort at NASA that we supported was a program developed at several centers called, *Rocket University*. Rocket U was designed to provide new hires experience in being part of a project team. Groups of young engineers were formed, and working with mentors, they had to start at the very beginning to learn how project management was done at NASA by developing and writing proposals for new products they wanted to design and build. It was a NASA version of *Shark Tank*, and they were required to present these ideas to NASA management. These could be almost anything, but the proposed project had to demonstrate some engineering or scientific results that would be useful to the agency. Once proposals were approved, the groups were mentored by NASA managers and engineers and were required to follow the very structured project management process that NASA has developed.

Each engineer was given an assignment as the project manager or systems engineer or lead mechanical or electronics engineer, and so on. In their new roles, they were required to design and build their product and to conduct the numerous project milestone reviews with NASA management.

Rocket U was a great learning experience for all of these young engineers. It demonstrated in a real-world environment how programs are conducted in our agency, it gave them the hands-on experience of assembling and testing hardware, and it developed the team building and communication skills they may not have received in their undergraduate education. It allowed them to hit the ground running when they were assigned to their first NASA project. I can remember their excitement when I was invited to a Rocket U team's sounding rocket launch at the Kennedy Space Center. These young engineers developed this hardware mostly on their own time, after work hours and on Saturdays. That's the kind of attitude and succession planning a KM program can bring to an organization.

In this chapter, you learned the following:

- Succession planning is critical to your organization's growth and stability. Knowledge management can play a critical and positive role in developing future corporate leaders.
- KM can also play an important part of onboarding new hires but introducing them to your organization's history and culture.
- Your lean KM program can also assist managers at the highest levels who may be facing critical situations by becoming a research office and the sharing lessons of the past by explaining how other managers facing the similar issues either succeeded or failed.

Questions to consider are as follows:

- Does your organization have a succession plan for critical corporate roles? If not, can you explain to upper management how KM can help?
- Any organization hoping to succeed is going to need to develop current employees into leaders. Can you explain why this is the perfect role for KM?
- Can you explain the benefits of incorporating KM, right from the start, for new hire training?

CHAPTER 9

What KM Can't Do

We've talked a lot about the value of KM and how it can help your organization, but let's be realistic and truthful with ourselves and look at the other side: what knowledge management cannot do.

Predict the Future and the "Unknown Unknowns"

During the height of the Iraq War, U.S. Secretary of Defense, Donald Rumsfeld, in response to a reporter's question, described the difficulties of developing strategy because of the, "unknown unknowns—the ones we don't know we don't know." Although this is a somewhat confusing exercise in semantics, in reality, it makes a bit of sense. There's a lot of stuff out there that you are simply unaware of despite your best efforts. Accidents are still going to happen, hopefully with your strong KM program in place, not the same ones that happened in the past. But new, *unknown unknowns* can occur, and a failure or mistake can happen.

In order to manage risk and avoid potential problems, we often try to predict what future problems may occur. Unfortunately, we generally tend to guess the most obvious events happening, which, in reality, seldom happen. Most problems that occur are the result of very complex systems cascading into an almost chain reaction. It's seldom a simple straightforward cause that can readily be predicted or forecasted. (As an example, take a look at the Concorde Case Study in Appendix B.)

Knowledge management's job is to develop a culture that understands there are *unknown unknowns* out there. Once you understand they exist, you can be as vigilant as possible to discover them before they create problems. KM cannot prevent the *unknown unknowns*; unfortunately, people, nature, and complex systems have a real knack for outsmarting even the best knowledge management programs.

Overly Complex Systems and Situations

When president Trump's senior advisor, Jared Kushner, was explaining to the Middle East expert and author, Robert Satloff, the administration's plans for creating peace in the Middle East, Mr. Kushner stated, "If we fail, we don't want to fail like it's been done in the past." Whereupon Mr. Satloff responded, "You want to be original in your failure?" Mr. Satloff is an expert on Middle East policy and diplomacy, and he is well aware of the incredible complexities involved in that area of the world and the countless failures in the past to deliver a lasting peace to the region.

Unknown and unclear causal effects are inherent with overly complex systems, and it can be extremely difficult to pinpoint what went wrong and what lessons can be gained.

Prevent Some Degree of Discomfort

A good KM program is, for the most part, based in a large part on a catalog of failures and problems. You are going to cause some typical human reactions of embarrassment and resentment because your program seeks to highlight their mistakes. But, unless you have transparency and approach KM as a tool for learning, and certainly not for shaming, you're not going to have a successful program. You should redact names, when appropriate, but you should also bring awareness that everyone makes mistakes and only those who learn from their mistakes will succeed. That's why, it is an important component of your program to foster a culture of transparency by looking at failure not as something that needs to be punished and then forgotten but looking at it from a different angle where failure is seen as part of the process to success. Rather than viewing mistakes as embarrassments, get people, especially upper management, to describe their *best mistake* made on their way to success. Henry Ford, who tried and failed several times before he became one of the greatest industrialists in history, understood the value of learning from the past said, "The only real mistake is the one from which we learn nothing."

Maybe There's No Lesson to Be Learned

Dwight Schrute, from the popular TV show, *The Office*, once told a co-worker seeking his feedback from a lost sale, "Not everything is a lesson. Sometimes you just fail."

Well, certainly, we should try to learn something from every failure, but perhaps, Dwight does have a point; sometimes, you may be stretching things a bit in hopes of finding a lesson to be learned. If you're a fisherman, you understand sometimes the fish just aren't biting despite using the right tackle and bait. Or, maybe you're a very cautious and safe driver, but the person swerving into your lane and broadsiding you isn't nearly as cautious. You reflect back, "What did I do wrong? How could I have prevented this?" Well, you did nothing wrong; the car accident was out of your control. Should your lesson learned be to become even more cautious? Should it be to never drive a car again because there are so many bad drivers on the road? Hardly. Dwight Schrute was right; sometimes, there's no real worthwhile lesson or knowledge to be gained.

Get the Credit It Deserves

We often concentrate on what's wrong in the world and the bad news that seems to be happening almost everywhere. There is a lot of good news out there; the only problem is that no one really has much interest in hearing about it. For some reason, the human nature is more interested in the train wreck than reports showing the train arriving at the station everyday right on schedule.

A good example of this can be seen with the International Space Station (ISS). The ISS is the most expensive and complicated project ever designed and built by humans. Nothing matches it, not the Great Pyramid of Giza, or the Great Wall of China, or even the Apollo Moon Landing Program. Then, why haven't you heard much, or anything about it? Because it has worked nearly flawlessly for over 20 years. No one seems interested in good news. And, unfortunately, your well-managed KM program that has been quietly saving your organization from failures and mistakes can find itself pretty much in the same boat as the ISS.

Your KM program may be so good that it does what it's supposed to do and does it often—prevents costly mistakes. Because of your hard work and diligence, you've developed a culture where learning lessons from the past has become so ingrained within your workforce that costly mistakes have been prevented without anyone really knowing it. Even though KM is the reason, no one becomes aware about its success. When a mistake happens, everyone hears about it. When a mistake is prevented, it goes unnoticed. KM works in the background. It's like in an old Cold War movie where the hero secret agent, working anonymously and behind the scenes, prevents the outbreak of the World War III, and despite saving humanity, no one ever hears about his crucial actions or recognizes his contribution. Not much you can do, except know in your heart that you're doing the right thing, and if mistakes aren't being perpetuated, well, that's proof enough you're doing a good job.

In this chapter, you learned the following:

- Lean KM can be a critical component in any organization's success isn't the cure-all elixir to solve every organization's problems. If you sell it like a panacea to your management, you'll never live up to expectations.
- There are outside variables and situations that, no matter how hard you look and learn the lessons of the past, can come out of nowhere to cause a problem. You can prevent what you know might happen, but particularly in complex systems, there's no way to prevent every possible mishap.
- Lean KM is designed to prevent costly problems from happening. A successful KM program may never get the credit it deserves because its success at eliminating problems tends to go unnoticed and unappreciated when everything seems to be running so smoothly.

Questions to consider are as follows:

- Do you understand the significant value lean KM can bring to your organization as well as its limits? Are you comfortable explaining realistic expectations for your organization's KM program?
- Is your organization involved in designing and developing highly complex hardware? Can you see what benefits lean KM might bring to the process? Can you envision areas, such as cutting-edge technologies or other unknowns, that may cause problems?

Afterword

There's an example used in the Chaos theory called the *Butterfly Effect*, and it describes how a tiny, almost imperceptible event within a certain setting containing a perfect set of variables can snowball and create massive changes. It begins with a lone butterfly flying along the Atlantic coast off of Africa where the cooler ocean air begins to meet the hot, arid desert air from the Sahara. As the butterfly flaps its small, fragile wings, it begins to mix a tiny portion of the dry hot desert air with the cooler humid air of the Atlantic. Before long, this almost imperceptible air movement begins to grow and become more and more unstable, and within days, it develops into a thunderstorm off the coast continually growing larger and larger. Within weeks, the result of the butterfly's gentle flap of its wings is being tracked by National Oceanographic and Atmospheric Administration's satellites as it grows into a massive hurricane halfway across the ocean steam-rolling its way toward the Caribbean and the coast of Florida.

NASA's overall budget for fiscal year 2021 was about $24 billion. Of that, approximately $10 million was used for knowledge management (KM) training and services. That means KM spending at NASA is approximately 0.04 percent of the NASA budget or, in other words, for every $100 NASA spends, about four cents is devoted to KM and training. Off hand, that may not sound like very much, but look what it can accomplish if it is spent wisely and creatively. A robust lean KM program needs strong direction, clear focus, and an understanding of what your workforce needs to be successful more than an overly generous budget.

The butterfly effect is similar to how a well-conceived, well-managed lean KM program can impact your organization. Your program doesn't need to be huge to make a huge impact on your organization. Your lean KM program doesn't need to be expensive because the knowledge you are gathering and sharing has already been paid for by your organization—they already own it—you're simply gathering it, organizing it, and finding the best way to get it to the people who need it.

Your lean KM program needs to identify its customers and build a knowledge program devoted totally to helping them do their jobs efficiently, effectively, and safely. If your lean KM program is simple and straightforward—nothing fancy and certainly nothing esoteric—you'll discover that your stakeholders will support it and your customers will want to participate and contribute. Once you've established your lean KM program, you can improve your organization's processes, financial health, employee morale, efficiency, and safety. Your lean KM program can have the impact of a hurricane and can even change the culture of your organization.

Since the early days of human spaceflight astronaut crews, families and friends would gather at an old, secluded beach house located on the Kennedy Space Center. Before their flight, they'd relax and say their goodbyes at a pre-launch cook-out. It was a tradition during the Space Shuttle era that each crew would bring an unopened bottle of wine and place it with their mission patch into a wine cabinet among the empty bottles of previous shuttle crews. Their bottle would be opened upon their return, during their post-mission celebration. Today, when visiting the astronaut beach house, you can see two unopened bottles in the wine cabinet—one from the Challenger and another from the Columbia crew.

Figure A.1 Astronaut beach house

Figure A.2 The wine cabinets, today, in the astronaut beach house

Lean KM at NASA has played a crucial role to make certain astronauts, their families, and the NASA workforce never have to experience the heartbreak of another preventable tragedy. Viewing two unopened bottles of wine that were never uncorked and never enjoyed with a toast by exuberant crewmembers celebrating a job well done is a sobering reminder for every NASA employee of the criticality of learning lessons from the past.

KM doesn't have to be *gasping for breath* or endlessly trying to justify its existence within an organization. I believe lean KM is the answer. It worked for NASA.

APPENDIX A

Suggested Lessons Learned Input Form With Example

Abstract

A short summary describing of the proposed lesson learned. This allows the reader to quickly determine if this lesson learned is applicable to his/her situation.

Consideration for strain relief on wiring bundles during the design phase is essential for product reliability and hardware robustness. Designers may be unaware that wires required for flight operations require heavy stainless-steel sheathing for electromagnetic interference (EMI) protection.

Suggested Key Searchable Words

This is necessary to make the lesson learned searchable in a database. Use as many appropriate searchable words as possible to ensure a reader may locate it.

Strain relief; bundling wires; wire sheathing; electromagnetic interference; good design practices.

Description of Problem/Situation

The who, what, why, when, and how concerning the lesson learned.

Designers may not realize that during the assembly process the wiring called out in space flight experiments require a covering of stainless-steel braiding for EMI protection. When all the wires and associated shielding are bundled and routed, it often becomes quite large and heavier than the designer anticipated. This can increase the risk of failure if the wire bundles are not properly mounted and secured with strain reliefs. The following figure shows such a bundle. Notice the entire bundle is held in place only by the solder connection to the electronic board, which is not designed to hold such a heavy load.

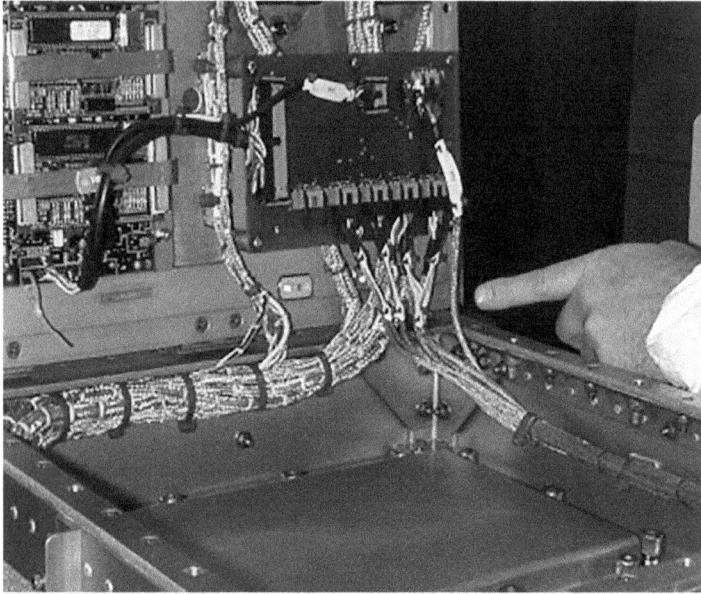

Wires/Strain Relief

Conclusion (How Problem/Situation Was Remedied)

The actions taken to solve the problem or issue along with recommendations to prevent its occurrence in the future.

Special brackets had to be fabricated and installed to provide proper strain relief for the wiring bundles. In the future, designers should be cognizant that all wires on flight projects require EMI shielding, which not only increases volume but also the weight of the bundles. Soldered joints are inadequate to support the additional weight. Strain relief components should be incorporated into designs.

The Concorde Accident: A Case Study

The Beginning of the End

In July 2000, at Houston's George Bush Intercontinental Airport, airline mechanic John Taylor riveted a 17-in. wear strip he had fabricated to a DC-10's General Electric CF6-50 engine. Taylor had difficulty positioning all the rivets and used aircraft mastic to help hold the wear strip in place.

A wear strip is a piece of sacrificial metal that acts both as a cushion and a tight seal for the engine's thrust reverser cowling. Replacing a wear strip is routine aircraft maintenance and is not considered a safety issue affecting operation or flight. John Taylor did not follow the manufacturer's recommendations when he fabricated it and decided to use a piece of titanium, presumably thinking that the much harder and stronger metal would last longer than the metal recommended by General Electric, the manufacturer.

At the time, he had no idea he would soon play a critical role in a chain reaction of catastrophic events. His titanium strip would be blamed for causing the world's most famous jetliner, the Concorde, to crash half a world away, contributing to the end of 27 years of commercial supersonic flight. Eight years after popping the last rivet in place, John Taylor would find himself facing manslaughter charges from a French court for the deaths of 113 people.

Overview of Concorde

Concorde was a joint engineering and project management effort between two historic rivals, the British and the French. It was the first attempt to realize the dream of supersonic commercial flight and an enormous engineering achievement for the time, considering the design and development began in the early 1960s. The project became an object of national pride for both countries, despite its agonizingly long development schedule and its enormous cost overruns. In 1976, when the Concorde made its first commercial flight to New York's JFK airport, the program was three years behind schedule and 15 times over budget.

Concorde Take-Off

Supersonic flight was nothing new, even in the 1960s. What was new was the length of time the Concorde would be required to fly at supersonic speeds. At the time, military aircraft had the capability to fly faster than sound but usually for only short intervals—to outrun an adversary or to dodge a missile. The Concorde was designed to fly at twice the speed of sound for its entire flight. For the London to New York flight, that meant flying supersonic for almost three hours.

Concorde was a technological marvel that, unfortunately, debuted its commercial service at exactly the wrong time. During her design, oil had been cheap, but after the Arab oil embargo of 1973, airlines quickly changed their purchasing requirements from increased speed to efficiency, creating a market in which the Concorde could never compete. Finding no buyers, the French and British governments, despite their enormous developmental investment, simply handed the fleet of 14 planes to their national airlines.

Concorde became a symbol of grace and luxury. Its iconic drooping nose and wide delta wing holding its four massive engines made her the most striking and memorable plane in aviation history. It catered to the rich and famous, those who could afford the astronomical fare (at times charging as much as $12,000 round trip) for one of the 100 seats on board, all of them first class.

But many people came to view the Concorde, not as a symbol of national pride and technological brilliance, but as a white elephant whose enormous developmental costs could never make commercial operation profitable. This brought public outcries that the poor were subsidizing the supersonic flights of the wealthy. Adding to this challenge, a new era of environmentalism began in the 1970s where Concorde's engines, with their huge black clouds of exhaust and deafening roar brought out just as many protesters as admirers to watch it take off and land.

The Concorde Design

All engineering involves compromise, especially when designing anything that moves. The faster it goes, the more compromises are needed. The Concorde was certainly no exception.

In order to achieve supersonic speeds, the British and French designers chose a huge fixed delta wing configuration. As military jet designers knew, a delta wing presented a formidable compromise because, although it would be quite efficient at supersonic speeds, it was incredibly inefficient at the subsonic flight speeds required over land as well as for take offs and landings. The wing also had to be rigid without any ailerons or flaps for control because any extraneous flaps would cause drag or be simply torn off at supersonic speeds. To control the pitch of the airplane while in flight, designers pumped fuel from one tank to another to distribute weight similar to early submariners who were required to run to the bow of their vessel to make it dive or to the stern to make it rise.

The fixed delta wing also required a very high angle of attack in order to take off. The Concorde's iconic stork-like stance placing the nose high above the tarmac was purposely designed in order to get the heavy aircraft with its fixed wing off the ground. The angle of attack was so steep that designers had to make the nose adjustable and swing downward on takeoff and landings so that the pilot could see the runway. They also had to install landing gear at the very rear of the fuselage so that the tail didn't scrape the runway.

The Concorde was fitted with four Rolls Royce Olympus engines equipped with afterburners capable of producing a combined thrust of 152,000 pounds at takeoff. The designers developed an ingenious computerized system of air intakes that reduced incoming supersonic airflow into the engines from 1,350 to 550 mph to reduce the risk of engine surge.

In order to feed these hungry engines, the huge wing also had to hold almost 31,500 gallons of jet fuel at a weight of 209,000 pounds. On average, the Concorde burned almost four times as much fuel per passenger as a giant Boeing 747 requires on a transatlantic flight. Required to fly at her inefficient subsonic speeds over populated areas to avoid creating sonic booms, she burned half her fuel by the time she reached Mach 2 over the Atlantic. The Concorde's four Rolls Royce engines could burn two tons of fuel just taxiing from the gate to takeoff—as much fuel as a modern Airbus 320 would burn flying from London to Paris.

As she taxied down the runway, with her Olympus engines roaring and afterburners shooting flames, the Concorde would move from 0–250 mph in 40 seconds—faster than a Formula 1 race car. With its fuel tanks full and a 100 passengers strapped in and their baggage stowed, the tires for the Concorde had to support the huge weight of the plane, as much as 408,000 pounds (204 tons), as well as higher than normal rotational speeds the Concorde delta wing required in order to get off the ground.

Once clearing land and heading over the ocean, the Concorde could finally make more efficient use of her delta wing and go supersonic at Mach 2 (1,354 mph)—faster than a rifle bullet. While over the Atlantic, the Concorde needed to reduce aerodynamic drag and flew much higher than subsonic flights (30,000 ft.) with her maximum altitude at 60,000 ft., almost 11.5 miles. At such an altitude, her passengers could see the curvature of the Earth out the tiny windows that had grown warm from flying at Mach 2. At this height, the Concorde flew above the Jetstream and any storms providing an incredibly smooth flight without any turbulence. Because she burned fuel so quickly ,the airplane continually became lighter, and the pilots had to re-direct the ballast fuel forward to keep her from continually climbing higher.

At such speeds, the Concorde's fuselage, and particularly its nose cone, grew very hot. The entire plane could grow over 9 in. during supersonic flight requiring the designers to equip her with expansion joints. The cabin floor was constructed on rollers to permit the expansion and contraction of the fuselage.

By the time the Concorde arrived in New York's busy airspace, she was seldom asked to go into any holding patterns and was usually given special treatment by air traffic controllers who knew at subsonic speeds she had to land ahead of others due to the inefficiencies inherent in her supersonic wing design.

The Concorde Disaster

Most engineering disasters, particularly those involving machinery with complex systems, seldom occur for just one major reason. Usually, there are a series of factors involved, leading to a cumulative catastrophic event. Such was the case on July 25, 2000, on Concorde Flight 4590 from Paris's Charles de Gaulle (CDG) airport to New York's JFK.

Flight 4590 was a chartered flight carrying a group of 100 German passengers to New York where they were to catch a cruise ship for the Caribbean and South American ports. With an impeccable safety record, Christian Marty was one of Air France's most talented pilots. But with today's flight almost an hour late and, knowing his passengers had to meet a cruise ship, the captain decided on expediency. Passengers on a chartered jet intending to go on an extended cruise are going to carry quite a bit of luggage, and the investigative report later stated that the Concorde was slightly overweight, beyond the recommended maximum structural weight of 408,009 pounds for flight.

Rather than burn extra fuel, Christian Marty decided to pump fuel toward the rear of the plane in order to shift the center of gravity allowing the plane to get airborne and compensate for the additional weight.

When Air France Concorde Flight 4590 left the gate and taxied to runway 26 Right, the flight controller told Marty that he had unfavorable tail winds at eight knots. For a plane on takeoff, head winds are preferred because they provide added lift, and this was particularly important for Flight 4590 because she was overweight. The extra weight along with the additional drag from head winds meant that Captain Marty would need most of the length of runway 26 Right during takeoff. But, in an attempt to get his passengers to their destination on time, Marty declined the opportunity to takeoff from another runway with a more favorable headwind.

As he was preparing the four Rolls Royce Olympus engines for full throttle, Captain Marty did not know that a Continental Airlines DC-10 had recently taken off from the same runway. Just minutes before, the DC-10 dropped mechanic John Taylor's makeshift wear strip on the same runway.

Typical runway maintenance at CDG called for three daily inspections to clean up any foreign object debris (FOD) that may have scattered on the runway. On this July afternoon, the planned inspection was canceled due to a routine fire drill.

As Captain Marty began to move the power levers to full throttle, he, as all pilots who flew the Concorde, was aware the sleek jetliner had a history of tire problems. Because of the extreme loads and speeds on takeoffs and landings, Concorde's tires were failing at a rate of one every 4,000 flying hours, 60 times more frequently than a typical airliner. In 1981, the U.S. National Transportation Safety Board (NTSB) expressed its concern over Concorde's recurring tire blowouts to Air France warning they could lead to *potentially catastrophic* results.

When Flight 4590 sped down the runway, her tires encountered the titanium wear strip that had fallen from the DC-10. Titanium, a very strong and tough metal, sliced like a razor into the tire on Concorde's left side. When the tire burst, large pieces of rubber flew at more than 300 mph, hitting the underside of the delta wing and firing like flak into the landing gear compartment, slicing through exposed hydraulic lines and electrical wires.

The largest tire fragment, approximately 4 ft. long and weighing more than 10 pounds, struck the underside of the wing hitting fuel tank number 5, which was completely full. As the tank was hit with such a violent blow, there was no empty air space in the tank to help absorb the hit. The tire fragment did not pierce the fuel tank, but caused a hydrodynamic pressure surge within the overfilled fuel tank. With nowhere to go, the fuel from inside tank 5 blew out an aluminum panel measuring about 1.5 ft. square of the underbelly.

Titanium Strip/Tire Fragment

As fuel began pouring out of the ruptured wing, the sparks from the torn electrical wires hanging from the wheel well ignited it. With the Concorde moving down the runway at such a high rate of speed, the fully engaged landing gear helped to slow down the flow of air, causing an almost perfect ignition sequence as the slower air atomized the fuel and sent the flames toward the engines.

Concorde Fire

Inside the cockpit the fire sensors were blaring and, instinctively, the flight engineer shutdown both left engines. Captain Marty had reached the speed where there was no turning back; the Concorde was running out of runway, and he had to take it airborne. Desperately trying to pull her nose up and hoping to make an emergency landing at a nearby airport, the plane struggled with the additional drag of the landing gear, as the pilots couldn't retract it due to the hydraulic leaks.

With its undercarriage ablaze, the Concorde never got above 200 ft. The pilots couldn't keep the delta wing airborne at such slow speeds, and she crashed less than two minutes after takeoff, barely six miles from CDG airport, hitting a hotel engulfing the area in flames. All 100 passengers were killed along with Captain Marty, his co-pilot, his flight engineer, six flight attendants, and four people on the ground at the hotel.

The Concorde Denouement

In many ways, the Concorde was ahead of its time. But with such a complex design, including so many innovative and pioneering features, it pushed the operational and safety boundaries of other critical subsystems. Her ingenious wing design allowed supersonic flight but with a compromise for the additional fuel and weight needed to fly her at subsonic speeds. The tire design during Concorde's operations couldn't reliably keep up with the demands for additional weight and the increased speeds required to get the Concorde off the ground.

But Concorde Flight 4590 also suffered from an almost inconceivable chain of events that all compounded into a catastrophe. Without one event in the series happening, flight 4590 may have arrived safely at JFK that evening and its passengers may have gone onto their Caribbean cruise. Certainly, John Taylor's decision to install a titanium wear strip was the easiest to blame, but there were other events and decisions that all contributed to the tragedy. For example, what if the runway inspection had been conducted and the titanium strip found? What if the wear strip had fallen flat on the runway allowing the Concorde tire to crush it rather than falling and landing upwards, like a knife blade? Or, what if John Taylor's wear strip had simply fallen a few inches to the right or left and Concorde's tire would have missed it?

What if Captain Marty, realizing his plane was overweight, had decided to burn off a ton or so of fuel while taxiing? Or, what if he had selected another runway without such a strong headwind? If he had done either, it's very possible the Concorde would have been airborne before hitting John Taylor's wear strip or had avoided it completely.

What if the NTSB or the British and French aviation safety commissions had placed the proper attention to Concorde's continual tire problems and grounded the fleet, forcing the airlines to work with manufacturers to develop a more reliable tire that could handle the speeds and loads?

Despite all the *what-ifs*, perhaps Flight 4590 was doomed long before it took off for JFK. Perhaps, the radical design of the Concorde was an accident waiting to happen. In this relation perhaps, the Concorde was similar in a way to the Space Shuttle, a vehicle that had always retained its designation as an experimental vehicle. Both were masterful designs, and because of their radical design, both carried significant risk.

Aftermath

After the crash of Flight 4590, all Concordes were grounded. British Airways and Air France made costly safety improvements such as lining all 13 fuel tanks with Kevlar and developing stronger tires less prone to blowouts and shredding. Charles DeGaulle and Heathrow airports instituted more rigorous runway inspections.

On September 11, 2001, British Airways was conducting a test flight over the Atlantic when the World Trade Center Towers were hit by terrorists. The *9/11 effect* killed the Concorde for good, as the world entered another economic slowdown and commercial travel, particularly business travel, came to a standstill.

Previous to Flight 4590, both British Airways and Air France boasted of the Concorde's safety record of flying almost three decades without an accident. In reality, the Concorde's safety record may not have been as stellar as advertised. The fleet of 14 Concordes never came close to logging the hours and number of takeoffs and landings of other commercial jet liners. For instance, during the same period that the Concorde flew, the huge international fleet of Boeing 737s would fly more hours in a week than the entire Concorde fleet did in their entire 27 years of commercial service. Judging the Concorde by the industry standard of *hull losses per million flights*, the crash of Flight 4590 outside of Charles de Gaulle Airport places Concorde's rating at 11.6, by far the worst of any modern jet liner.

The Concorde was pressed into service because of political pressure. The French and British governments were desperate to see it fly to justify its enormous developmental costs, as well as to foster a feeling of national pride in the world's only commercial supersonic airliner. But both British Airways and Air France were hampered by Concorde's massive maintenance and operating costs and could never make a reliable profit from her tickets.

In its 27 years of commercial service, the fleet of 14 supersonic jetliners that had carried more than two million passengers on champagne-filled flights across the Atlantic was now disbursed to museums around the world. In the United States, there are Concordes on display at the Smithsonian's Udvar-Hazy museum near Dulles Airport, aboard New York's Intrepid Air and Space Museum (along with the Space Shuttle *Enterprise*), and a third at Seattle's Museum of Flight.

In 2010, 10 years after the crash, a French court found mechanic John Taylor and Continental Airlines guilty of involuntary manslaughter in the deaths of 113 people. Two years later, a French appeals court exonerated Taylor, stating that the titanium wear strip did in fact lead to the accident, but that Taylor's poor workmanship was not criminal because no one could have predicted such devastating results. French Judge Michele Luga stated, "…he (Taylor) could never have imagined a scenario where this simple titanium blade could cause such a disaster." Afterward, Taylor mentioned to a newsman that the entire experience "…had ruined my life."

Additional Resources

The Federal Aviation Administration's Lessons Learned Air France 4590. https://lessonslearned.faa.gov/AirFrance4590/Concorde_Accident_Report.pdf

The French *Bureau Enquêtes-Accidents* Interim Report. https://bea.aero/docspa/2000/f-sc000725ae2/htm/f-sc000725ae2.htm

Chittum, S. 2018. *The Last Days of the Concorde*. Smithsonian.

About the Author

Mr. Forsgren started his career as a mechanic apprentice at NASA's Glenn Research Center in Cleveland, Ohio, and after 10 years of night school, earned an undergraduate and then graduate degree in engineering. In 2005, Mr. Forsgren transferred to NASA Headquarters in Washington, DC, to manage agency training efforts, and in 2013, was appointed the Director of the Academy of Program/Project and Engineering Leadership (APPEL). In 2016, he was given the additional responsibility of serving as the NASA Chief Knowledge Officer until his retirement in 2021. He and his wife live in Indialantic, Florida, and have four sons and four grandsons. Mr. Forsgren can be contacted at rforsgren4@gmail.com.

Index

OTHER TITLES IN THE PORTFOLIO AND PROJECT MANAGEMENT COLLECTION

Timothy J. Kloppenborg, Xavier University and
Kam Jugdev, Athabasca University, Editors

- *Moving the Needle With Lean OKRs* by Bart den Haak
- *Project Management for Banks* by Dan Bonner
- *HybridP3M* by Lukasz Rosinski
- *Successfully Achieving Strategy Through Effective Portfolio Management* by Frank R. Parth
- *Be Agile Do Agile* by Vittal Anantatmula and Timothy J. Kloppenborg
- *Project-Led Strategic Management* by James Marion, John Lewis, and Tracey Richardson
- *Workplace Jazz* by Gerald J. Leonard
- *Stakeholder-led Project Management, Second Edition* by Louise M. Worsley
- *Hybrid Project Management* by Mark Tolbert and Susan Parente
- *A.G.I.L.E. Thinking Demystified* by Frank Forte
- *Design: A Business Case* by Brigitte Borja de Mozota and Steinar Valade-Amland
- *Discoveries Through Personal Agility* by Raji Sivaraman and Michal Raczka
- *Project Communications* by Connie Plowman and Jill Diffendal

Concise and Applied Business Books

The Collection listed above is one of 30 business subject collections that Business Expert Press has grown to make BEP a premiere publisher of print and digital books. Our concise and applied books are for…

- Professionals and Practitioners
- Faculty who adopt our books for courses
- Librarians who know that BEP's Digital Libraries are a unique way to offer students ebooks to download, not restricted with any digital rights management
- Executive Training Course Leaders
- Business Seminar Organizers

Business Expert Press books are for anyone who needs to dig deeper on business ideas, goals, and solutions to everyday problems. Whether one print book, one ebook, or buying a digital library of 110 ebooks, we remain the affordable and smart way to be business smart. For more information, please visit www.businessexpertpress.com, or contact sales@businessexpertpress.com.

www.ingramcontent.com/pod-product-compliance
Lightning Source LLC
Chambersburg PA
CBHW061334220326
41599CB00026B/5178